Very often, women of color and women who know God find themselves at odds with the forces that seek to deny their personhood and shut them out of their God-ordained future. Dr. Deborah Wortham, with God's help, fought to become the gift to the world that God created her to be. Her reflections on her journey through loss, change, and trouble reveal her wisdom and strength. Her fierce determination to define herself and her refusal to allow anyone to do it for her should be an inspiration to all.

~ Rev. Dr. Elaine M. Flake

SETTING
THE
ATMOSPHERE

BELIEFS, PRACTICES, AND PROTOCOLS FOR FAITH-FILLED EDUCATIONAL LEADERS

SETTING

THE

ATMOSPHERE

BELIEFS, PRACTICES, AND PROTOCOLS FOR FAITH-FILLED EDUCATIONAL LEADERS

by:

DR. DEBORAH L. WORTHAM

VINE
PUBLISHING

Vine Publishing's name and logo are trademarks of Vine Publishing, Inc.

ISBN: 979-8-9867471-7-0 (paperback)
ISBN: 979-8-9867471-9-4 (e-book)

Library of Congress Cataloging-in-Publication Data
Library of Congress Control Number: 2023905389

Published by Vine Publishing, Inc.
New York, NY
www.vinepublish.com

Printed in the United States of America

DEDICATED TO THE MEMORY OF:

Leon and Bessie Smith
Loretta Diane Smith
Leon C. Smith, Jr.
Shakira Smith
Roosevelt and Mintha Summers

May their inspiration for life and learning perpetuate the future.

CONTENTS

ACKNOWLEDGMENTS

There is an anointing required to transform schools, and therefore I want to start by thanking the One who has anointed me to do this work, the Almighty God. To my beloved husband, Chester, thank you for always supporting, believing, and encouraging me to tell my stories. You're my rock. To my children, Dr. Shelley Connell and Chester III, you are my inspiration. To my brother, Phillip Smith and sister, Dr. Audrey Donaldson, it is our sibling rivalry that has kept me moving forward. Exon, Porcha, and Michael, continue to follow the path that Mimi prayed for. To my favorite grandchildren, Jordynn Lynn, Chester IV, Sheldon Jr, Zachary, and Ethan, you are "fearfully and wonderfully made." With the favor of the Lord and the right atmosphere, nothing can stop you.

Thank you to God's messengers who have stood tall and prophesied that I would write books that would transform the world. To Pastor, the Rev. Dr. Elaine Flake, thank you for always making me feel like I was the only member out of twenty thousand. Bishop E. McD. Wortham, thank you for your prayers, guidance, and gentle prodding to go deeper, do more, and "never run to the fire; let God handle it." Thank you to everyone who has poured into me and empowered me to pour into others.

To every staff member, student, Board member, and community member that I have had the privilege to serve over these fifty years, thank you from the bottom of my heart. Thank you to everyone who has played an instrumental role in my life and career. I'm forever grateful.

INVOCATION

O h, Ancient of Days, I humbly pray this book provides wisdom, guidance, strength, and precious development time to pedagogues tasked with leading, teaching, counseling, and nurturing children. May the words contained within, augmented by prayer, meditation, sacrifice, and lived experience, help readers find their best selves in and out of the classroom. May principals be guided by principles that show how the whole can be greater than the sum of its parts. Bless sisters and brothers who are assiduously working to plant seeds of possibility, resilience, hope, and perseverance in the hearts, minds, and spirits of their young charges and adults in and out of the school, not for selfish motives or vain ambition but out of a deep and abiding response to their calling. Let this thought, "Never allow personal smallness to get in the way of spiritual greatness," be a lesson that is taught, embraced, and shared. May readers discover the power behind moving toward a shared vision instead of fighting to escape the debilitating quagmire of acrimonious division. May the author's words be heard as pragmatic and spiritual creations rather than recited recitations. May the hearts and minds of superintendents be quickened by the fire needed to ignite institutional and systemic change that can lead to transformation rather than grow content presenting rehashed 'changeless change' theories and practices as the next new thing. Oh Lord, pour out a special blessing over the households of educators; protect their children and their children's children and loved ones as they wage war against the destructive forces that come to steal, rob, and destroy. Look in on warriors who may have grown weary by the constant and ever-pressing battle to continue to show up by refreshing their mind, body, and soul. You said in your Word,

Behold, I will do a new thing, now it shall spring forth; shall you not know it? I will even make a road in the wilderness,
and rivers in the desert.

We sit in our tent door, ready to embrace a new thing. I close this prayer with this scripture taken from Psalm 78: 1-4:

My people hear my teaching;
listen to the words of my mouth.
I will open my mouth with a parable;
I will utter hidden things, things from of old—
things we have heard and known,
things our ancestors have told us.
We will not hide them from their descendants;
we will tell the next generation
the praiseworthy deeds of the Lord,

his power, and the wonders he has done.

.   Amen.

-Rev. Dr. Alfonso Wyatt

Public Theologian, Educator, Mentor

INTRODUCTION

Oprah Winfrey's *Live Your Best Life* tour was in full swing, and I knew I had to be there. When the tour dates were announced, I quickly went online, only to discover that there was only one ticket left for the New Jersey venue.

"This is mine!" I thought and so I hurried, entered my credit card information, and purchased the ticket. "Ah!!! I can't believe it! I got the last ticket! Thank you, Jesus!" I screamed. This ticket was not only for a first-row seat, but it also included lunch with the Queen of Media herself, Oprah! I was excited, to say the least!

Sitting among other attendees in an intimate atmosphere with Oprah was a dream come true. As we sat there, we were given index cards in preparation for our one-on-one meeting. One of the questions Oprah asked was, "What do you want to accomplish in life?" My response to her was, "I want to publish a book and tell my story about being called to serve as an educational evangelist." Upon giving her a synopsis of the book, Oprah replied, "Wow!" She then referred me to her writers and publishers, who reached out to me for several years following that amazing day. However, I believe that God's timing is the right timing, and now I'm ready to use my experiences, stories, and voice to help leaders set the atmosphere.

Setting the Atmosphere means creating an intentional culture where systems of beliefs, practices, and protocols work in tandem to educate the whole child. These systems, when implemented, permeate every decision in every classroom, and every office. Superintendents, principals, and teachers know too well the fragmentation that exists in the absence of these systems, and that is why I wrote *Setting the Atmosphere: Beliefs, Practices, and Protocols for Educational Leaders*.

This book is an experiential guide, written for educational leaders who are passionate about teaching, leading, and empowering learners. It is unique in that it is written in the voice of my relationship with Almighty God. As an educational evangelist, my faith is at the core of all that I do. As such, scriptures are coupled with real scenarios, practical approaches, and effective strategies for leaders to create, support, and sustain systems that cultivate an atmosphere for successful leadership and student achievement.

Setting the Atmosphere is broken down into three sections: Belief Systems (cultivating a faith-filled mindset), Practices (effective methods that yield favorable results), and Protocols (sustainable systems for current and future achievement), each of which demonstrates approaches for identifying and overcoming obstacles commonly faced when manifesting an atmosphere crucial for success. Each instructional narrative is filled with wisdom, guidance, and a time for reflection.

As you read this book, take the time to reflect on your school's and/or district's mission, vision, values, and goals. Use the space provided to note your thoughts, and if necessary, do the work to realign yourself and relocate processes to your settings. It is my prayer that as you navigate through the pages of this book, you will be strengthened, encouraged, enlightened, and inspired by the vignettes and strategies provided. May my experiences and transparency be a guiding light, providing insight and a blueprint for leadership designed to enhance a positive culture, a growth mindset, and an environment where all are successful.

PART 1

THE BIRTH OF AN EDUCATIONAL EVANGELIST

1

FROM DEBRA TO DEBORAH

I was the Mother's Day baby, or so I thought. For most of my life, I believed I was born on Mother's Day in 1949. I was the fourth of five children born to Leon and Bessie Smith, and I was my mother's favorite. With a loving gaze, my mom would consistently look into my eyes and exclaim, "Oh Debra, you are my Christian child, born on Mother's Day."

On the other hand, my siblings would always say, "Oh, you just think you're special because you were born on Mother's Day," and truth be told, I thought I was! At least, I thought I was my mother's gift on Mother's Day, until 2005.

I remember the day like it was yesterday. I was now an Assistant Superintendent of a school district in Maryland. Back then, Blackberry phones were the new tech gadget for corporate America. Every executive had one, and so did I. My BlackBerry allowed me to do more than I could on an average mobile phone, including the capacity to view calendars from previous years. So, one day, as I was becoming acclimated to the new phone, I thought, *I should look up my birthday. After all, I was born on Mother's Day.* I began the process by navigating through the screens, moving from one year to the next, and eventually got to the year 1949. Slowly, I moved from month to month, day to day, and finally arrived on May 13, 1949. "Friday?! I thought my mom said I was born on a Sunday! Friday?!" I was in disbelief. I was shocked! I was not my mother's "Mother's Day gift."

My first thought was to call my mom. "Mom, I thought you said I was born on Mother's Day?" "You were!," she said.

"Mom, I'm looking at this Blackberry, and it says I was born on a Friday."

"That's the devil!," she replied. "Put it down!"

The initial shock wore off, and what I realized then was my mom's determination to shield me from the belief the world held regarding *Friday the 13th*. She did not want me to be associated with the negativity of that day; she did not want me to be labeled the "unlucky Friday the 13th child." Instead, she created a positive narrative that set the atmosphere of my life and positioned me as a unique gift to be cherished.

My mom, Mrs. Bessie E. Smith, did her best to set the atmosphere for all her children. She was a strong woman of faith who taught us how to love the Lord, love learning, and have a deep, abiding love for family. When I look at the life and legacy of my mom, I think of the lessons she taught us. Through her, I learned how to face challenges with faith. No matter the circumstance, she would listen, pause, and then say, "Can you see Jesus?" Through her, I learned to value education as a means of independence and success. Through her, I learned the importance of "mother wit"—good common sense. She would always say, "Birds of a feather flock together" and "You are known by the company you keep."

My parents were instrumental in the development of my value system. My father instilled in us the importance of having a good work ethic. He led by example, and I looked to both parents to shape my growth and development as Debra Smith—that is, until my introduction to Deborah, the judge and the leader.

Growing up, I've always loved God, and my faith was of the utmost importance. I was that child who always wanted to go to church. Each week I looked forward to attending Sunday School at the Christ Temple Cathedral, Holiness U.S.A. I loved the Lord; I even wanted to be a nun at one point. For me, nunship meant that one was *special*; *chosen*, and who doesn't want to be special and chosen by God?! I was set on joining the Sisters at the Catholic Church right across the street from my elementary school.

One day, in the coat room, a kid said, "You know that nuns aren't allowed to get married or have children, right?"

"What?! Oh no! I'll pass," and with that, my preteen dream of becoming a nun was over.

Fast forward to my teenage years, and while I was like any other all-American teenager, dealing with the challenges that come with teen growth, my relationship with God was still very important. I wanted to spend time with friends, but I also wanted to spend time with God. And so, each day, I would carve out some time to pray and study God's Word. It was during one of those study times that I came across Judge Deborah, one of the most influential women in the Bible. Known for her wisdom, courage, and faith, Judge

Deborah was a prophet and the only female judge in the book of Judges. She was a powerful woman of God who heard God's voice and shared God's Word with others. And to top it off, she was a wife and a mother! I was fascinated with her life, her story, her contribution as a community leader, her obedience, her courage, and her truthfulness. Deborah was the embodiment of leadership at its finest, and I wanted to be her. "I think I'll change the spelling of my name! Instead of spelling it Debra (as stated on my birth certificate), I'll spell it D.E.B.O.R.A.H. Yes, DEBORAH, that's who I am!" I wanted to embody her traits and reputation, and so from that moment on, *Deborah* was written on every paper and on every document—anything that required my name or signature.

Deborah was a part of me, and I strived to be her throughout my life. I had to draw on her courage, strength, and obedience when my oldest sister Lori was diagnosed with multiple sclerosis, and I, for some reason, was the person who had the lead position of taking care of her. I didn't participate in after-school activities (with joy, truth be told); instead, I ran home to take care of my sister. I never questioned why. I knew I had to be obedient to my assignment of caring for Lori.

As a senior, I accepted an invitation to tour the University of Wisconsin in Madison, Wisconsin. When we were scheduled to leave, my sister Lori was extremely ill. My family and I gathered for a family meeting, and my sister called me to her bedside during our time together. She took my hand and said, "If you decide to go to the University of Wisconsin for college, promise me that you will be the best you can be." "I promise!" Truthfully, I did not know what it meant to "be the best you could be," but I figured we would talk about it when I returned from the tour.

When I arrived in Wisconsin, I saw buildings, ice cream, and an abundance of cheese. I knew this was the place for me! Out of thirty-five thousand students, only fifty were African Americans. The University of Wisconsin offered 5-year scholarships to African American students because they believed we could not graduate in four years. Regardless of what they thought, my mind was made up. This was my college of choice.

The tour ended, and I was excited to go home to tell my sister Lori about my college decision. As I entered the house, it looked like a holiday. It looked like Easter, Thanksgiving, or Christmas. Family members from everywhere gathered in the living room. They were seated on that, *oh, you better not sit on the white sofa with the hard plastic covering* couch. I thought they had all gathered to hear my college decision. After all, attending college was expected of every family member on both sides of my family. However, it only took a few seconds to realize they were there because my sister Lori had gone on to be with the Lord. I was heartbroken. I would never have the opportunity to find out what her instructions meant, but I held it close, never forgetting her words. I no longer had my sister here on earth with me, but I had her in my heart as I continued the journey from high school to college and beyond. I also still had Deborah with me, my biblical mentor.

Courage, obedience, and truthfulness carried me through my

college years at the University of Wisconsin, which changed my life. On the first day of college, I met Chester Wortham (who would later become my husband). I majored in Education, and I lived in an all-black dorm during my first year on campus. In my second year, I lived in Lowell Hall, an all-Jewish dorm. That was an experience that I will never forget. In my third year, I lived in an apartment off-campus. And year four? I lived at home to serve as an intern in Downers Grove, Illinois. One of the best parts of my program was the reward it offered to the top 10% of the graduating class. Those students had the opportunity to serve as interns throughout the United States while receiving 50% of the teacher's salary. And guess what? I was one of those blessed students. I became a member of Alpha Kappa Alpha Sorority, Inc. during my junior year. By year four, my journey with the University of Wisconsin was complete. Upon graduation, I married my husband, pursued a Master's degree, and a Doctorate in Educational Leadership, all while embarking on a career in Education.

I've always been passionate about education. With all its experiences, life gave meaning to Lori's last words to me, "Be the best you could be." I now understand what it means to *be the best; to be a blessing; to make the best effort to help others and do my best to serve.* Education has given me the platform to do and be my best. If you are reading this, you are most likely an educational leader, and therefore you know the daily difficulties educators face. But, as I look at my life and career, I'm grateful that I can draw from the knowledge imparted to me by my parents, my sister's encouragement, and Deborah's biblical traits. No matter the challenges I have had to face in all the roles I've served in as a Teacher, Assistant Principal, Principal, Director, Assistant Superintendent, and now Superintendent, I've held on to the fact that God did not give me a spirit of fear, but of power and of love, and of a sound mind (2 Timothy 1:7). Daily I walk in Godly courage—charting new territories and taking bold steps to change schools and lives. Despite the challenges I faced, teaching, organizing, and mentoring, I held on to my belief that "obedience is better than sacrifice" (1 Samuel 15:22), so I chose obedience—listening for God's guidance in all things. When I walked the hallways, met with faculty, sat with parents, and fellowshipped with the community, I would put on the *belt of truth*, knowing that opposition would come and challenges would occur, but once I lived in and by truth, all would work out for good.

Today, I believe I'm where I'm supposed to be. I'm called to serve, empower, uplift, encourage, and educate. God, my faith, my parents, my sister, Judge Deborah, and all my experiences have birthed me as the Educational Evangelist—a zealous advocate for the development of others—one who sets the atmosphere where all students, faculty, and educational leaders can flourish and thrive.

"For with God, all things are possible." (Mark 10:27)

PART 2

BELIEF SYSTEMS

This first section is comprised of stories highlighting the importance of developing a belief system. No matter who you are and where you are in your educational journey, we all can agree that the mind is powerful. It dedicates our vision, and it directs us emotionally and even physically. In other words, how we see a person or a thing determines how we show up, how we interact, and what we do. As such, the very first thing we need to address is your belief system— the foundational truths that drive you, sustain you, and help you to set the atmosphere.

2

YOUR FAITH MATTERS

I was a new teacher at school number 86 in Baltimore, Maryland, and I was excited about the opportunity to teach. However, I first needed to get my class list from the secretary.

"Thank you, Mrs. M," and off I went with my first teaching assignment. But, as I began to look at the list, I thought, "Oh no, Mrs. M. must have made a mistake! Every student in this second-grade class is reading at a readiness level! No, she made a mistake. I think I'm supposed to be teaching first grade." I was convinced, so I made my way back to the principal's office. All she had to do was fix it—that is, change the words "second grade" to "first grade" on my list, and I would be good to go. "This is an easy fix!" I thought.

The conversation went like this: "Good morning, Ms. Jenkins. I have discovered a slight error. My class list says I am teaching second grade, but all the students read at a kindergarten level."

Ms. Jenkins, taller and slightly wider than I was, looked at the list and then looked at me and said, "There's no mistake. The students are in the second grade!"

Shocked and confused, I responded, "What am I supposed to do? They are nowhere near second-grade reading level."

She replied, "Teach them!" She looked at me with the look that only your mother gives when she is about to knock you into next year if you say another word!

"Okay," and with that, I slowly walked out of her office with my second-grade list in hand.

I was distraught, to say the least. I needed guidance and knew I could get it from my bishop. So, that Tuesday evening after Bible study, I waited patiently to speak with him. I waited as person after person greeted him and shared a testimony—some good news about what God did, how God turned things around, and how God showed up for them and their loved ones. Everyone had a testimony, but I didn't; I had a lament! I wanted to tell the bishop about the principal. Finally, it was my turn to speak.

"Bishop, the principal gave me a class list, and all the children are well below reading level. I thought someone made a mistake and gave me the wrong grade level for the class!"

Bishop looked at me with the same look Ms. Jenkins gave me, except this time, I didn't feel like he would knock me into next year. He said, "Well, Sister Wortham, you might as well...teach them."

I gasped. Did he just say what Ms. Jenkins said to me?! With eyes wide and mouth opened in disbelief, I pulled myself together and politely responded, "Okay, Bishop," and I turned and slowly left the building. I drove home incensed.

Well, that didn't work. The only thing I had at that moment was my faith. I knew I needed to rely on God like never before. So, I relented and decided to change my perspective on the situation.

Instead of seeing it from a "doomed to fail" lens, I began to see it as a "faith challenge—an opportunity for God to "show up and out" in the situation. *Deborah, do you believe God can do this through you or has it all been lip service?* I had to believe.

It was the first day of school. As each student walked into the classroom, they each gave me a look that translated to, "Do you know I can't read?" Without a word coming from my lips, I responded, "I know, but it's going to be all right." I was up for the challenge. I tapped into my relationship with God, trusting that God would lead and that God did. One of the divine inspirations given to me was the use of hand signals. This was not something I had done before, but one day I began using hand signals with each skill I taught. Combining the hand signals with the new skill lessons enabled students to grasp the concept and learn the meaning. Each time we did it, their confidence grew, and they were on fire. Honestly, I didn't even have a name for my new teaching strategy. I just knew that I had surrendered this class and my capacity to teach to God in prayer. I later discovered that these hand signals were called mnemonics—a strategy that helps students remember important information.

I made it through an entire school year with this second-grade class, and at the end of it, the lowest reading level in that class was third grade (on average), and the highest reading level was 12th grade (on average). God is faithful! This first successful teaching assignment marked the beginning of my exodus from the classroom. The School Board heard about the test scores and visited my class. They could not believe what they saw and what they heard. There were forty students in the class with seventeen independent groups—students working collaboratively and small and large group instruction—all with just one teacher...me! We used the 1/3-2/3 model. Following that model meant the teacher directed instruction for 1/3 of the class time, and the students worked in small groups for the following 2/3 of the period. This model allowed for differentiated instruction while exercising a belief that all children can learn when we teach them how to learn. The model and the use of mnemonics worked, but what I discovered during that time was the importance of my faith. Today, I stand flatfooted on the belief that when God calls you, God will equip you. Where is your faith?

LEADERSHIP CORNER

You may be just embarking on your career as a teacher, or perhaps you are stepping into a new role—you've accepted a new assignment, know that your faith is required. The doors that will be opened to you, and the opportunities ahead will require a deep conviction that your help comes from a Divine source. One can always try to figure it out by oneself, but it's easier to trust God and tap into your faith.

Leadership Lesson: Faith matters, and when you tap into it, God will give you the creativity and capacity to succeed.

Scripture Support: *"Now faith is the assurance (title deed, confirmation) of things hoped for (divinely guaranteed), and the evidence of things not seen [the conviction of their reality—faith comprehends as fact what cannot be experienced by the physical senses]." Hebrews 11:1 (AMP)*

3

FAILURE IS NOT AN OPTION

"See this face?! This face is not wearing a uniform!" The star quarterback shouted during a listening tour organized to gauge the students' expectations. As the new superintendent, I knew that uniforms were a board policy and a non-negotiable for all students. I also knew that this student's outburst would influence the student body, as he was considered a leader among his peers. So, instead of responding, I retreated to my office to call his mother.

"Mrs. Wilson, thank you for coming in. We'll get Sean. I want him to be in this meeting."

Sean entered my office surprised and confused. "Why is my mother here?" But, before I could respond to his question, he ran to my bookshelf, and with amazement in his eyes shouted, "It's a book! It's a book! See!" He rolled up his sleeves, "I have it tattooed here! "Failure is not an option!" This young man not only had the words tattooed on his arm, but he embodied the belief that with hard work, success was achievable.

"Well, you know, I wrote a chapter in that book!" I told him.

"What?! No! That's so cool, Dr. Wortham!" In that moment,

Sean and I bonded over a shared belief system. We both believed that failure would never be an option.

These five simple yet powerful words have undergirded my initiatives throughout my career. No matter the challenges, I believed. Like Sean, I believed that with hard work and dedication, success was inevitable. At the core of this belief is my faith in God, who has equipped and called me to be an educator. As educational leaders, we must believe that we are chosen by God to make a difference, and if so, we are equipped to succeed. When we do our best each day to be informed, prepared, and committed, then God will do the rest. Daily, when faced with challenges, we must ask ourselves, "Do I believe?"

Failure is not an option. It is with this belief that I have been able to serve districts that others have deemed irreparable and transform schools, students, and communities. It is with this belief that district after district moved from "school improvement" to "good standing." It is with this belief that I have been able to succeed against opposition, step into uncharted territories, innovate, and navigate through difficult times. This belief that failure is not an option has allowed me to discover the tools and strategies necessary to educate the whole child.

Not only should we hold tightly to this belief, but is also important that we impart this belief to our students and faculty. The belief systems of both students and faculty are pivotal to the overall success of the district. Each individual must believe that, with hard work, success is inevitable. As educational leaders, failure is not and should never be an option. We do not have to have those words tattooed on our arms like Sean has, but we should have them tattooed on our hearts. With every school, with every student, with every interaction, with every district, and with every challenge, we must believe in our hearts that success is possible.

LEADERSHIP CORNER

A shared belief system among students and, more importantly, among faculty, is instrumental in setting the atmosphere. It is the faculty that conveys the belief system that sets schools up for success or failure. It is our responsibility as educational leaders to sow the seeds of success by operationalizing the belief that failure is not an option.

Leadership Lesson: Failure will never be an option when you have cultivated a winning mindset.

Scripture Support: *But Jesus looked at them and said, "With people [as far as it depends on them] it is impossible, but with God all things are possible." (Matthew 19:26 AMP)*

4

VISION BEYOND WHAT YOU SEE

I was one of three assistant principals assigned to work with a principal (I'll refer to him as Mr. Sam) for one of the largest elementary schools on the East Coast. Mr. Sam served as an excellent leader and mentor on this journey. If you knew Mr. Sam, you knew him as humble yet highly regarded throughout the country for his leadership style. I will never forget one nugget he shared with me. He said, "Deborah, you can catch more bees with honey." Although not original, it resonates with me to this day. I, along with the other assistant principals, appreciated Mr. Sam's wisdom. We all worked together, doing our best to support him and ensure the school's success, but we all knew that at some point, we would have to transition from assistant to principal. However, since I had only been in that school for one year (typically, one would need to serve for two years in that school before principalship), my next steps were not at the forefront of my mind—I was happy to serve in the capacity of Assistant Principal.

On the other hand, Donald had just completed his second-year tenure as an Assistant Principal. It was hard to fathom Donald leaving because he became my prayer partner as we shepherded 1,700 students to their next level. Donald exemplified the importance of relationships, and everyone respected his leadership. We learned the merit and worth of collaboration and the resulting effort in student achievement. But we knew the day would come for his assignment as principal.

Then, it happened. While gathered in Mr. Sam's office for our morning meeting, the telephone rang.

We heard Mr. Sam say, "Oh, he is? Oh, OK. He is right here."

Mr. Sam beckoned Donald to the phone. I tried to figure out what was happening by attempting to read his face, but he was expressionless. We could hear Donald say, "Oh, I am. Oh, Thank you." When he hung up the phone, we learned that Donald was appointed Principal of the lowest-performing school in the state. Upset and confused, he began to question the assignment.

"Mr. Sam, whom did I offend at Central Office? What did I do wrong?"

We all stood there...silent. What could one say? Donald was trying to make sense of it all. He could not fathom that this would be his next assignment. Mr. Sam had no answers and could only shake his head. We all stood in place, thinking of the right words to say. No one left the room. What we envisioned to be a celebratory moment felt like a funeral—it felt like we were all mourning.

Then, the telephone rang again. Donald was summoned to the phone.

He said, "Hello. I'm not? She is?" Then he turned and said, "Deborah, telephone." Donald chuckled as he extended the phone to me, and Mr. Sam stood frozen in time as he had not received any additional information. Slowly, I turned, and step by step, I drew closer to the phone.

As if in slow motion, I took the phone from Donald. My voice became weak as I identified myself to the caller. The next words I heard were, "You are appointed Principal of an Elementary School."

"What? How did this happen?!" Donald was no longer assigned to the lowest-performing school in the state; I was! He received an assignment to a brand-new school, for which he had to attend the ribbon-cutting ceremony. There was no ceremony for me. Suddenly, with one phone call, Donald was no longer mourning; I was.

What did I do wrong? Who did I offend? These were some of my first thoughts. The questions ensued, but even as I wondered what went wrong, deep within my spirit, I could hear, "I can do all things through Christ who gives me strength" (Philippians 4:13). So, after a few minutes of getting over the initial shock, I shifted my perspective and saw this as an opportunity to *set the atmosphere*—to take control of my head, heart, and mind.

Donald and I were now assigned as principals, and our duties began that same day. We both left the office not knowing what we would face as principals. Donald left and went to his ribbon-cutting ceremony, after which he offered to drive me to my new school, which was not too far from Martin Luther King, Jr. Boulevard. He pulled up to the school, and immediately drove off the minute I exited the car. One could probably still see the tire tracks left by how fast he drove off! I stood there on the grounds of my new elementary school. As I looked, I could only see the bars on the windows, and my first thought was, "What are they trying to keep in, or what are they trying to keep out?" Standing alone in the foyer, I closed my eyes and prayed for divine help. At that moment, I was reminded that *it was not about me!*

As I opened my eyes, God gave me the vision to see what I did not initially see in the natural. I saw a beautiful foyer with historically exposed bricks. Although all 700 students lived in either low-rise or high-rise subsidized housing, I saw a "rich" environment with grass instead of concrete, much like in high-income areas. I saw a marble floor (albeit under twenty years of wax). God opened my eyes to see the future rather than the facts of failure presented. God gave me the vision to see beyond the reality presented to me.

This vision was what I needed to serve these students and the community. It took some time and hard work, but I kept the vision before me. That summer, I had to deal with issues of transition and staff changes like a revolving door, but I kept sight of the vision. So, instead of doing what many others would have done, I instead opted to hire half of the staff from the non-traditional path, that is, alternatively certified teachers. The experience allowed me to witness the importance of passion in fulfilling your purpose. These teachers had a passion and learned the process and product of teaching. It was an extraordinary leadership and learning experience. The leadership team responded to the clarion call that beckoned "servant leaders."

We were committed to "setting the atmosphere" mentally,

physically, and spiritually. We were cautious and conscientious about our words, knowing there was power in the words we spoke. We sowed into the restoration of the building. One day I asked the custodians to provide me with bleach and ammonia. Little did they know I mixed them to restore the marble floor in the foyer. Yes, the result was the release of gas. And no, I wouldn't recommend anyone to do this. But I so wanted the vision that God gave me to manifest that I took it upon myself to do the work (I cleaned without the help of the custodians). At the end of my private DIY project, I was overwhelmed by the toxic combination and had to go to the hospital. But, again, while I probably wouldn't have exposed myself to those toxins in retrospect, I was happy with the results—beautiful marble floors. Did the end justify the means? Not necessarily, but that's the power of vision—it drives us to do whatever it takes for its manifestation.

The journey to school improvement continued with systems for being healthy, safe, supported, engaged, and challenged. For four years, I served this school while holding on to the vision God gave me on that first day. At the end of my tenure, the school received America's Best School Award for Significant Improvement. What began as a daunting assignment became an opportunity to cultivate vision. Regardless of the challenges I faced as the school's principal, I understood that we would be lost; without vision, we were destined to fail. But with divinely inspired vision, prayer, and faith, we were able to transform the lives of hundreds of students. What do you see?

LEADERSHIP CORNER

Vision is the capacity to see beyond your current reality. You may serve in a low-income community, and everything around you seem hopeless, but this is your opportunity to cultivate vision. Ask God to open your eyes to see what you cannot see. Ask God to open your eyes to see new possibilities and to give you the wisdom to execute the vision. Remember, a vision is what you and your school district hope to become.

Leadership Lesson: Vision is the catalyst that propels your leadership. Open your eyes to see what others cannot see.

Scripture Support: *"For we walk by faith, not by sight [living our lives in a manner consistent with our confident belief in God's promises]." (2 Corinthians 5:7 AMP)*

5

HOW DO YOU SEE THEM?

In January of the school year, I was asked to become the principal of a large high school that had lost its status as one of the top ten schools in the state. When the position was offered, I asked the superintendent why she chose me.

Dr. Albert responded, "You know how to rally the troops."

What does that mean? I thought. "Dr. Albert, other former high school principals work in the central office. Why didn't you choose one of them? I've only been a principal of an elementary school and an elementary/middle school. What experience do I have for high school?"

Dr. Albert looked at me reassuringly and said, "You know how to bring people together and change systems to work effectively for staff and students." Before I could respond, and not taking no for an answer, Dr. Albert continued, "With a Doctorate, we would take your pay scale to the highest in the district."

I smiled and thought, *Hmmm, it's not about money. However, that's an incentive!* "So, when do you want me to start?"

To my surprise, Dr. Albert responded, "Tomorrow." Anyone

who knows me knows that self-care and grooming are important to me. So how could I start this new position without a trip to the salon?!

"Dr. Albert, I can't start tomorrow. I need to get a manicure, pedicure, hair 'did', etc!" But she needed me to start immediately.

I was already working as the Director of Professional Development for 250 schools and 85,000 students. How could I possibly do both jobs? So, I asked her, "How will I be able to do the work I'm assigned to do as the Director of Professional Development?" I was trying to figure it all out.

"There is a conference room across the hall from the principal's office," she replied. "Hold your meetings and run the District's Professional Development Department from the conference room."

"Oh, okay." And with that, I accepted the position.

The next day I arrived at the school, and with tears in my eyes, I walked down a long hallway toward the principal's office. The security guard asked if he could help me because I looked lost. "Yes, where is the principal's office?" I was grateful for his direction because I had no idea where I was going and had so much on my mind. I believed that my steps were ordered by the Lord, and the long walk down the hall allowed me to commune with God. As I spoke with the Lord, I envisioned a giant blackboard suspended from the ceiling with the words "Leadership is Leadership" written on it. I was flooded with peace and renewed confidence. I knew at that moment that I was not alone. I knew that provision had preceded me, and God would help me do the work to set the atmosphere for success in that school. That was the message I needed to assume the Principalship of a failing high school. After all, I received an award for creating America's Best Elementary School for Significant Improvement. However, I knew I couldn't rest on my past laurels. The message was clear, "Leadership is Leadership."

As I prepared to enter the principal's office, I saw a sign on the door that said, "Do not enter! Please see the secretary for an appointment." At that moment, I understood why it was important for the superintendent to find someone who could "rally the troops." When I think about it now, I wish I had saved the sign because it's a reminder to build relationships and not create a barrier between you and others.

I started my tenure as the principal of a 1,200-student body, determined to see the school differently. On the first day, I walked from classroom to classroom, encouraging the young people who sat in the hallway, cutting class. When I saw them sitting in the stairwells with the smell of marijuana, I didn't judge them nor did I reprimand them, I only said, "Where are you going to college?" They all looked at me as if I were crazy, but I wanted them to know I saw them. I saw their potential. I saw what they could be. I saw their greatness. "I can't get you to where you need to be. I can't get you from here to there. Come, go with me to class." And with that, they got up and walked with me to their classroom.

That morning I journeyed to each classroom, going in and introducing myself. After all, no one knew that a new principal was assigned to the school. "Good morning. I'm Dr. Wortham, the new principal."

The response was, "She's cute!"

"And you, dear student, just earned an A!" This is off to a good start! The students had question after question: *Are we going to see you? Are we going to see you at our games? Are we going to see you in the cafeteria?* I initially thought, "Why would I go to the cafeteria when I heard about the food fights?" But then I thought about it again and knew that the solution was changing the atmosphere in the cafeteria—new tables, chairs, a new look, a new feel, and a new lunch schedule; a change that would make the students feel seen. And yes, I ate with them many days without food fights.

As I made my rounds as the new principal, I noticed that most students wore their coats throughout the day. Even though it was mid-January and cold, I thought it was strange, so I implemented a rule that upon entering the school, all students must put their coats in their lockers. I figured this would fix the problem, but it did not. In each class, there they were, students with their coats on.

"Ugh, is my tenure going to be a tug-of-war with these students?!" I had to think of something. I eventually asked the custodian to install hooks in my office. When students were seen in their coats, I would take them and place them on the hooks in my office. I was sure that confiscating their coats until the end of the school day would deter them from disobeying my "coats in the locker" rule. But it did not! Instead of deterring the students, they voluntarily hung their coats in my office.

My office became the coat room! Now, at first glance, one

may see these students' actions as insubordination, but at a second glance, I saw students who needed a solution. They refused to put their coats in their locker because there weren't enough lockers. My office became their coat room, and further allowed me to build relationships with the students.

Each morning as they hung up their coats, they would greet me, "Good morning Dr. Wortham!" and I would respond with, "Good Morning, young woman or man!" These exchanges taught me to look beyond the seeming insubordination of the students to see the root of the issues.

It was also crucial that the staff knew that I saw them and that their presence and voice mattered to me. So, one of my first initiatives as principal was to gather my troops of staff for a meeting to gauge their thoughts on what was working and what wasn't in the school. Each received a card that read "Go" on one side and "Stop" on the other. The meeting was successful, as the staff felt heard and seen. The meeting created a bond between me and the staff. In essence, there was a buy-in…a buy-in of the vision to get the students from "here to there."

Day after day, and month after month, I continued to serve. I attended basketball games consistently, only to end up refereeing "love birds" snuggled up in the bleachers. Once it was clear that we were here to cheer on the team, the snuggle ended. Eventually, I stood at the door that led to the locker room, where the team retreated during halftime. I would stand there and high-five each player, encouraging the team to win. And that is what they did. Game after game, they won! The only game that I was not present for was the qualifying playoffs. On that day, I had a speaking engagement out of state. The students were devastated. So, what did they do? They blew up a picture of me and pasted it next to the door, where I would typically stand to give them a high five and encouraging words. They did this because they knew I saw and believed in them, and guess what? They won and moved on to the championship game. Not once did students ask me about my credentials! Not once did students ask me if I knew the Pythagorean theorem. They didn't care about my degrees. They only cared about my presence. They cared because I cared.

As the school year ended, I thought about how it began. It began with losing its status as one of the Top Ten High Schools in the state for performance and concluded with being "Restored to the Top Ten." In June, 300 out of 301 students graduated and received acceptance letters to college. What happened to that one student? He decided not to let his parents see him walk the stage. So, he attended the graduation but served as the photographer. He received his diploma in August. But, as I stood there, beaming with joy at the students' graduation, I was glad that I had said "Yes" to the position despite my concerns and, most importantly, despite the external noise—the naysayers, the doubters, the folks who did not believe that I could do the job successfully. I am glad I blocked out the noise and focused on God's voice. I was glad that God gave me the vision to see the school and the students as successful, even when everything seemed contrary.

Dr. Albert offered me an Assistant Superintendent position after my tenure at this high school. When I asked her why the offer was for Assistant Superintendent of high schools, she responded, "You sat among your colleagues, and you were successful. You have their respect, and that is what we need." My thought is, "Leadership is Leadership!"

LEADERSHIP CORNER

You may be assigned to a failing class or school, but how do you see the opportunity before you? How do you see the school? Do you see it as others? Do you see the potential that's within its walls? How do you see the students? Do you see them as failures, or do you see them as accomplished and successful? Remember, what you see is connected to your belief system, the psychological foundation for setting the atmosphere. Ask God to help you see the school and students differently.

Leadership Lesson: How you see them will determine how you show up for them.

Scripture Support: *"See that you do not despise or think less of one of these little ones, for I say to you that their angels in heaven [are in the presence of and] continually look upon the face of My Father who is in heaven." (Matthew 18:10 AMP)*

6

THE ESTHER EFFECT:
MAKING DECISIONS FOR THE GOOD OF THE MASSES

"I guess all your experience prepared you for such a time as this," said a colleague during a phone call. I felt like Esther, now facing a crisis of epic proportions. What was that crisis? It was the COVID-19 pandemic. Much like Queen Esther (Esther 4), I was now tasked with leading a district through a life-and-death situation. There were no rulebooks for a pandemic—no historical records, policies, or procedures to guide us when students and staff alike tested positive for the virus. Like the Jewish Queen, sitting back and not being proactive when lives were at stake was not an option.

When there were no answers, I had to implement the Esther-Effect—leading through crisis with faith, insight, courage, and determination. I had to first rely on my faith—my belief system. While I did not immediately have the answers, I believed that humanity's extremity is God's opportunity. In other words, I firmly believed that, though devastating, this pandemic was an opportunity for God to show His power on earth. My faith and belief were grounded in my conviction that God could and would birth insight for a strategy of safety.

Insight in the midst of a crisis is manifested through collaboration, revelation, and wisdom. It was while talking with others, including the assistant superintendent of Human Resources, that I discovered that we could legally close schools on Monday and Tuesday, using our two leftover snow days. In addition, it was while talking with a nurse, whom I considered an *angel nurse*, that I discovered that we could use "star days." At the time, I was not familiar with this term, but upon further inquiry, I learned that "star days" were three days during spring break that allowed districts to close schools during any emergency. The plan began to take shape, but much like Esther, approval from a higher authority was needed.

As leaders, we must not be afraid to go against the status quo. I first needed to get the Board's approval to implement those "star days," but once we did everything within our power, we needed more. As I thought about how God, through faith and collaboration with others, gave me a strategy for school closures and the safety of staff and students, I knew that the wisdom I had needed to be shared for the good of the masses. It was not enough for my district to have a plan, I had to share this plan with state leadership.

"Deborah, you have held your peace long enough. You must save your people, and if you don't speak up now, who will?!" My thoughts raced as other superintendents, and I met with representatives from the entire state. Unlike the other superintendents in the room, my district had exhausted all possibilities and needed state intervention. So, I slowly rose to my feet with the courage and determination to ensure that all would be safe. "I am the first district in the state to have three students test positive for COVID-19. We have used all our star days, as well as our snow days. We need the state to give us the jurisdiction to close the schools." I felt like Esther, standing before the king, and like Esther, my voice was heard, and my request was granted.

Perhaps I was sent to serve that district for such a time as this. Other districts were able to look to my district for a roadmap for moving through the pandemic and ensuring the safety of the masses. As educational leaders, you will have to face a crisis or two, or three during your career. However, when you employ the Esther-Effect—when the good of the masses fuels your actions, and you lead with faith, insight, courage, and determination, you will succeed in setting and maintaining the atmosphere.

LEADERSHIP CORNER

If you haven't already, as an educational leader, you will be tasked with making decisions for the few or for the masses. Much like Esther, you must employ faith, insight, courage, and determination. The crisis you are facing or will face may not be a global pandemic, but all decision-making processes must be undergirded by collaboration, revelation, and wisdom. How can you apply the Esther-Effect as a leadership strategy?

Leadership Lesson: Know when to speak up, shut up, show up, partner up, and pray up.

Scripture Support: *"For if you remain silent at this time, liberation and rescue will arise for the Jews from another place, and you and your father's house will perish [since you did not help when you had the chance]. And who knows whether you have attained royalty for such a time as this [and for this very purpose]?" (Esther 4:14 AMP)*

7

FROM A FIXED MINDSET TO A GROWTH MINDSET

What does it feel like the morning after your budget fails? It feels like you want to avoid getting up and going to work. *Deborah, the Lord is your strength.* The budget failed not once, but twice, and to top it off, we were one of only three districts out of 700 that had to deal with the disappointment of a failed budget. As the superintendent, this situation makes the headline news, the Commissioner calls to encourage you, and all you feel like doing is giving up. You just want to take a pill and make it all go away. *Deborah, hold your head high, and don't let them see you sweat. Keep moving forward. Remember, you are here to serve the children.* There are so many challenges I've had to face throughout my career as an educational leader, but when one has a growth mindset, the response to failure differs.

A fixed mindset is one that sees challenges as limitations and barriers to success. However, I believe that a growth mindset is one that views challenges as opportunities for growth that become the catalyst for future success. A growth mindset is rooted in faith and trust. So, the budget failed, and we had to rely on a contingency budget, but I was determined to present my best and to keep the children at the forefront of my mind. I trusted and had faith that everything would work out. My years of experience taught me that a failed budget is only the result of a deeper, long-standing issue within the community, one that had to be addressed. *Deborah, stay focused. This is an opportunity, not a barrier.*

When the budget fails during the public board meeting, it can feel like a walk of shame, but I believed God. So, I sat there throughout the meeting with my shoulders up and my head held high. Despite a failed budget, the evening turned out to be a win for me and my district. First, we won the budget video award, which meant that our community outreach was successful and effective. This was a huge win for us because there were 511 entries, and so to be recognized by the New York State Public School Relations Association as worthy of winning the first prize spoke volumes. We were elated, to say the least.

The second win of the night came when test scores for grades three through eight showed an increase in scores for ELA and math. This meant that the district's beliefs, practices, and protocols were effective, and students were achieving on a higher level. Finally, the third win for the night was when an external audit revealed that our district, for three consecutive years, ended the year in the black. This was another huge win because that added $245,000 to our fund balance. The budget failed, but I walked out of that meeting ready to take a victory lap. As a superintendent, I knew that the issues that prevented the budget from being passed could not prevent us from being victorious because we were diligent throughout the year to set the atmosphere for students and staff to flourish and thrive.

LEADERSHIP CORNER

As mentioned, a failed budget is usually about something other than the budget. It is usually a long-standing issue that did not develop overnight. Look at all the issues surrounding the district. What is the elephant in the room? It is the elephant in the room that prohibits the passing of the budget. When you have and maintain a growth mindset, it is your positive response to something negative that allows you to walk with your head held high. So, how can a growth mindset help you through some of the challenges that you are facing or will face?

Leadership Lesson: A fixed mindset creates limited results, but a growth mindset yields huge dividends.

Scripture Support: *I can do all things [which He has called me to do] through Him who strengthens and empowers me [to fulfill His purpose—I am self-sufficient in Christ's sufficiency; I am ready for anything and equal to anything through Him who infuses me with inner strength and confident peace.] (Philippians 4:13 AMP)*

8

REACHING HIGHER HEIGHTS

I believe that Barack Obama, the first African-American president of the United States, served during a time of exciting shifts in the field of education. He believed that education was the pathway to secure a better future, and as such, during his tenure, he laid out a series of challenges for the nation to meet. Those challenges included initiatives in job training, and as well as programs that were designed to increase the college attendance rate.

In a letter penned to his daughters during his presidency, President Obama highlighted his desire for his daughters' education. Upon reading this letter, I was inspired to push the boundaries for students and adults to secure a better future.

In an address to a joint session of Congress, President Obama presented his educational plan, which would result in the United States ranking first in the world for the number of college graduates. He urged individuals with no high school diploma, to do the necessary work to obtain it, and those with a high school diploma, he encouraged them to pursue higher levels of education by going to college or undertaking some sort of career training. All his initiatives and plans undergirded his belief in reaching for higher heights, and as I listened, read, and gleaned from his leadership, I welcomed the challenge.

As educational leaders, we are uniquely positioned to help make the United States the number one leader in education a reality. Yes, becoming the world leader in college graduates will require hard work, but we can do this if we believe in "setting the atmosphere" and reaching for higher heights. In order to do this, our belief system must be centered on three key areas:

- **Desire**: We are called to help students cultivate a vision of a future that is successful through education. We are called to help our students envision a life that is fulfilling, purposeful, and driven by the knowledge that they have the capacity to succeed. We are in a position to inspire our students, so that they can have the desire to reach their ultimate goal.

- **Discipline**: As educational leaders, we must model and instill the importance of a disciplined life by being committed, focused, and having a strategy for success. Through this process, which is based on hard work, students will excel.

- **Dedication:** As educational leaders, we must instill the law of completion. Dedication means winners never quit, and quitters never win. Students' efforts should not culminate in a series of incompletes. They must not be an almost.

Accepting the challenge of the President's narrative became my narrative, and I did my part to rally the troops to implement the directive. I believed in the President's message. It resonated with my heart and influenced my decision-making process. Having delivered the President's address almost daily, it became my leadership language. I knew what the atmosphere looked, sounded, and felt like, as well as the steps to reach higher. So, when I was asked, along with other educational leaders, to have lunch with President Obama to discuss the impact of education, I was honored and excited, to say the least. Attending the luncheon allowed me to recite my acquired leadership language in the presence of the architect himself, President Obama. I memorized my presentation, and I was ready! At the conclusion of it, I will never forget how he stood with his arms folded in amazement. I will never forget the look on Congressman Elijah Cummings' face as he watched me, his mentee.

A few years later, when former President Obama hosted a *My Brother's Keeper Summit* in my state, I received a call from an official at the Department of Education stating that they would include our graduation rate progress in the address to the President. This moment was a full-circle moment for me, and one I will never forget. Years after adopting his directive during his address to the joint session of Congress, I had mastered the art of reaching higher heights, and the work was now institutionalized and recognized nationally. To God be the glory!

LEADERSHIP CORNER

Maintaining the status quo is never an option. As educational leaders we must strive to reach higher heights. However, our efforts must be willful, planned, and systemic. Reaching higher heights is not accidental; it's intentional.

Leadership Lesson: Believe in your capacity to soar.

Scripture Support: *Apply your heart to instruction, and your ears to words of knowledge. (Proverbs 23:12 (NIV)*

PART 3

PRACTICES OF AN EFFECTIVE LEADER

Effective educational leadership is one that uses transformational strategies and develops essential systems for the success of students and the betterment of the community at large. The following stories highlight practices that I have implemented throughout my tenure as an educational evangelist and leader. Glean from my experiences and consider the best practices that work best for the institution(s) you serve.

9

EFFICACIOUS LEADERS

The COVID-19 pandemic took us all by surprise. There were no rulebooks on what to do in the midst of a pandemic. There was no expert, or pandemic consultant that we could call on to help us figure things out, especially when 140 staff members were absent. There was no "pandemic administration 101" class that educational leaders could take. No matter our leadership role, we all had to learn on the go, and pivot and re-pivot at any moment.

That pandemic taught us the importance of God's presence. When we were isolated, away from loved ones, and feeling lonely, God's peace and presence were needed more than ever. God was and continues to be my strength and joy—the One who reassures me of His unchangeable goodness, limitless power, and sustaining grace. I needed God…we needed God to help us make it through that pandemic. We learned that God was our Source, but we also learned the importance of being efficacious leaders.

Efficacious leaders are leaders who have the confidence and faith to get the job done. However, they are those who recognize they do not have all the answers. They are leaders who are not bound by obstacles. They are those who are open to listening, learning, and relearning. They are those who realize that what may have worked in one period of time, may not work in another. They are those who are not stuck in what is but look ahead to what could be. They are administrators, teachers, vice principals, principals, assistant superintendents, and superintendents who are open and willing to change. Educational leaders must employ the practice of being efficacious leaders.

I had to be open and willing to change through the most difficult time in education. Managing hundreds of staff and students during a major crisis required that I admit I didn't have all the answers. I had to learn new techniques and strategies in my effort to keep students engaged through online learning. I had to recognize that classroom instructional techniques did not work with online instructions. I had to learn how to keep both staff and students safe. When day after day, and week after week, news, and policies were changing, I had to believe, adapt, and move swiftly with the changes. I had to learn new technologies and new ways of communicating. The pandemic reminded me to remain hungry for knowledge and to be eager to grow.

As educational leaders, let us continue to employ the practice of being efficacious. Take a continuing education class, attend a seminar or conference, receive feedback as an opportunity for growth rather than criticism, and be open to new ideas and ways of doing things. Don't be quick to dismiss someone you may assume does not have the same level of education. We can learn from everyone if we are humble enough to do so. When we remain open and faith-filled, we will be able to set the atmosphere for success even in the midst of a pandemic shutdown. Let us all commit to consistent learning and growing, only then will we be true leaders who successfully set the atmosphere.

LEADERSHIP CORNER

Don't let a crisis like a global pandemic stop you from being an effective leader. Efficacious leaders stay ahead of the curve because they are consistently expanding their wealth of knowledge. Take advantage of a crisis and use your resources. Today, decide to open your mind to new ways of serving the schools and students you have been called to serve. The reality is that it is so easy for you to remain in that place of comfort and familiarity—to keep doing the same thing day after day without any thought of change. But there is so much more that you can do—so much more than you can achieve. Think about it—in what ways have you shunned new ideas and strategies? How can you be open and efficacious? What does efficacious leadership look like for you?

Leadership Lesson: Efficacious leaders are led by humility, curiosity, and a desire to grow.

Scripture Support: *"Do nothing out of selfish ambition or vain conceit. Rather, in humility value others above yourselves, not looking to your own interests but each of you to the interests of the others." (Philippians 2:3-4 NIV)*

10

BONDING VITALIZERS

It is often said, "Practice makes Perfect." While I believe that the adage is true to a point, I would append it to say, "Perfect Practice Makes Perfect." I believe that "perfect practice"—that is, perpetuating correct strategies over a period of time—will yield to the perfection of leadership excellence. A shift in the culture is possible when collective, collaborative practices are initiated, implemented, and institutionalized. When a *practice* is institutionalized, leaders will not have to negotiate or renegotiate contracts; one will not have to make an official declaration. Institutionalized practices will be received as policy and become a habit of the mind. Practices are governed by and for the people collectively.

In leading staff, governing schools, advocating for students, and monitoring the systems, beliefs, and protocols of institutions that I have had the honor to serve, I've come to understand the role of inter-teacher connections, and vitalizers in effectively setting the atmosphere.

INTER-TEACHER CONNECTION:

The bond among staff is critical to the health of the institution. The bond must begin with the core leaders and critical messengers, that is the superintendents and principals. Superintendents must create safe, empowering spaces for principals to be heard and given the tools for success. Principals must create safe, encouraging spaces for teachers to be heard and revitalized. I like to say it like this, "Feed the teachers, so they don't eat the children." This means build teachers' confidence; lavish them with words of encouragement, affirmation, confirmation, and redirection. To lavish teachers means undergirding their efforts through thought, words, and deeds. When teachers feel seen, heard, and fed daily doses of positivity, they won't "eat" the children—they won't stifle their voices, destroy their dreams, and devour their hopes for a bright future.

Staff must know that leadership cares, but staff must also care for one another. Strife breeds toxicity and creates an unhealthy culture. Whether or not we realize it, students pay attention to adult interactions around them. Students' academic achievement suffers when there is fighting among staff and negative energy. As such, providing safe spaces for grievances to be heard, reconciliation to take place, and bonds to be strengthened is essential.

As an assistant superintendent, while conducting a professional development session at a low-performing school, I overheard a teacher say, "She wants us to bond, and we don't even like each other." My first thought was, "This 'us against them' mentality is one of the reasons why this school is not doing well. There is no unity." As leaders, we must do the work of unifying those we are called to lead. Yes, there will be misunderstandings, miscommunications, and perhaps, even offenses, but principals should implement pragmatic strategies that heal the divide and strengthen the bond. A few practices may include:

1. Creating opportunities for teacher collaboration. This may include relocating teachers to foster interaction and eliminate isolation.

2. Creating opportunities for teachers to conduct inter-room visitations to exchange successful strategies and provide encouragement.

3. Creating opportunities for departments and grade-level staff to convene and convey creative constructs for the forward movement of staff and students.

Finally, when we think about creating a bond using various elements, the first thing we think about is the means by which parts will be held together. Will we use nuts and bolts? Will we use super glue or Elmer's glue? If the adhesive does not work, what do we do? Typically, we go back to the instructions, and if that does not work, we replace it. Now, while this is only an analogy, what do you do if someone on the team refuses to bond? We should always ascertain whether or not they followed the directions and/or the group norms. If they did not and will not, then perhaps it's time to replace them. I believe that we need 75 percent of the building to move together, heading towards collective success. The other 25 percent will get on board or leave. Know your 75 percent, work with them, and move forward.

VITALIZERS

Vitalizers transmit energy and spirit using common language, verbal and nonverbal, as well as practices that unify and ignite the atmosphere. This means that leaders must embody the same energy and spirit that they are endeavoring to transmit. They set the standard and expectations for the atmosphere. Vitalizers maintain control, inspire the body towards a common goal, and impart a spirit of diligence, excellence, and belief. Here are a few practices that a vitalizer may incorporate.

1. *Calling the Atmosphere to Order:* I can't emphasize enough how important it is to foster and maintain an orderly atmosphere—whether it is in the cafeteria, classroom, auditorium, or on the school bus. Any place where students and faculty are gathered, leaders must know how to quiet the chatter and call the atmosphere to order. There have been many times when I have used the practice of call and response to rally everyone and command attention. As the superintendent of the Roosevelt school district, I've stood in the midst of everyone present and, with all my energy, belted out, "Roosevelt!" The response was a loud echo, "Rising!" This call and response set the atmosphere to order and ignites confidence in who we are as a community. At the start of a middle school Parent-Teacher assembly, I stood on the stage and calmly said, "1, 2, 3" to approximately 700 students. The students responded, "S-h-h-h-h-h!" quieted

themselves, and turned their attention to the speaker. After the assembly, a parent approached me and expressed how impressed she was by the fact that the students immediately focused their attention upon the initiating call. She was so impressed that she told her son that she would use the call and response signal at home and expected the same respectful, responsive result. Calling the atmosphere is a practice that all must be coached to do. All educational leaders must develop the skill of creating and commanding the atmosphere.

2. *Nonverbal Communication:* There is so much that we can say without saying it. Using nonverbal communication as a vitalizer affirms and reenergizes students and staff. During the pandemic, I encouraged what I called "eye hugs"—eye contact with quick blinks that communicated care without the need to touch. A simple smile, a joyful gasp, and a soft clap (as if attending the Master's Golf Tournament) communicate approval of a job well done and keep the blaze of confidence aglow. Nonverbal communication begins the second a leader enters a space. Our body speaks. Our energy speaks. Our presence speaks. Speak life without words. Speak assurance without words. Speak confidence without words. Set the atmosphere with and without words. Your nonverbal communication matters.

3. *Teachers' Presence Outside the Classroom:* A great vitalizer is what I call The Gathering—encouraging staff to meet students in

the hallways, outside the classroom during class transitions. While serving as a high school principal and the Area Superintendent for 24 high schools, we began standing in the middle of the hall during class transitions. Our presence did several things:

- It created a space for faculty and students alike to bond beyond the classroom. Teachers were not standing there like hall monitors, but it was an opportunity for them to engage, give a high five to a student or co-worker, inquire about a student's well-being, and so much more. We demonstrated the ritual of a family reunion, and an atmosphere of admiration, caring, and hospitality was fostered in the hallways as students and teachers saluted each other.

- Staff presence among students in the hallways prevents a breach in the atmosphere. Their presence helps to prevent negative energies and behaviors from interrupting a synergistic atmosphere that was set for the purposes of learning, collaboration, and connection. This offensive stance is not possible by simply being an observer standing in the doorway of one's classroom. Educational leaders must be in position—be active participants, with the understanding that their presence makes a difference.

Daily connectivity practices and vitalizers that create bonds and charge the atmosphere will yield environments that foster cooperation, emotional support, and personal and collective growth.

How do you deal with internal conflicts among those you are called to lead? What bonding practices do you have in place? What vitalizers can you put in place to energize students and staff alike? As leaders, we should constantly monitor our environments, ensuring that bonds are secure, and that toxicity isn't seeping through unmonitored cracks.

Leadership Lesson: Inspect, fix, and recharge the atmosphere.

Scripture: *Make every effort to keep the oneness of the Spirit in the bond of peace [each individual working together to make the whole successful]. (Ephesians 4:3 AMP)*

11

FROM STATE TAKEOVER TO GOOD STANDING: HOW TO MAKE THE TRANSITION

I accepted an assignment as the principal of a K–8 school in Maryland, following the conclusion of my assignment as the Director of Efficacy. On my first day at the school, I was greeted by a welcoming committee of one. Lonnie was a tall, handsome student who was waiting for me right by my parking spot.

"Is you the new Principal?," he inquired.

I looked at him, a bit bewildered, trying to figure out how to respond. Do I respond with, "I am," "I is," "I was," or "I be!"

He continued, "If you is, I want you to know that I am smart and not bad!" I was intrigued. As I made my way toward the school entrance, Lonnie felt the need to inform me about how he was viewed by the school staff.

"The teachers in that school don't believe in me. They think I cause trouble and don't do my work. They suspend me all of the time!" Having heard an earful, I invited him to walk with me as I entered the place that "didn't believe in him." Lonnie's welcome was unexpected, but the conversation stirred up everything I believed about teaching and learning. All I could do at that moment was reassure him that things would change.

I finally reached my office, placed my purse on the desk, and just then, I saw a letter from the State Secretary of Education. Alarmed, I tore the envelope open and read the letter. While I can't remember every word, I remember the word "Reconstituted." It was official…I was now the new principal of a school that the State Secretary of Education had placed on notice. In Maryland (at that time), if your test scores decreased for three consecutive years, you were "Reconstituted." Not only was my school warned, but eighteen additional schools in the district received the same letter, and we were all assigned to the same Assistant Superintendent. We all felt "banished" from the district. The letter was clear, "You have one year to improve student achievement, or the school will be Reconstituted…that is, taken over." Suddenly, everything that Lonnie said came back to mind, "Perhaps what he said was true!" I had one year to help this school transition from failure to *good standing*.

It would be foolish to keep doing the same thing and expecting different results. We could not remain the same. This would be a challenge; however, within our cohort, we were committed to increasing student achievement. The school improvement process was collaborative internally and externally. Together, based on data, we birthed a whole school reform process. We rallied teams comprised of staff, students, and the community. Community engagement was at peak performance. Students' voices were anticipated and heard throughout the school improvement process. Lonnie? His voice took center stage.

Through communication with staff and reviewing records, I found that Lonnie had an IEP and was enrolled in a self-contained class. I made a commitment to him and his family that, with hard work, he would exit special education. Lonnie worked hard and became my "unofficial assistant principal." He knew the entire student body, and they respected him. If Lonnie said, "Wear your uniform every day," they did.

Teacher collaboration and creating professional learning communities became assets in identifying a whole reform model. Staff selected the Johns Hopkins "Success for All" reform model that focused on balanced literacy, intense professional development, and monitoring. We also implemented half-days off for students on Wednesdays to afford the time for staff professional development. Additionally, our K–8 school embraced the "Success for All" model, with a deep commitment to the efficacy philosophy—the belief that self-confidence leads to effective effort (commitment, focus, and strategy) and yields success for achievement.

The reform process mimicked strategies that helped maintain high-performing schools while shifting low-performing ones. These strategies included:

1. Job-embedded Professional Development
2. Collaborative Institutionalization of the Mission and Vision
3. Commitment to Instructional Leadership
4. Focused Learning Walks
5. Observation, Evaluation, and Feedback

Our efforts to move the school from "Reconstitution" to "Good Standing" yielded favorable results. When two teachers came to my office and inquired what they should do when students were not on grade level, my haste to dismiss their question became the significant instructional component: "Teach them all on one grade level, then differentiate in small groups." Student achievement levels increased in the first quarter of the year. This caught the central administration's attention, and as a result, the "teach and then differentiate" model became the instructional model for the district. Ultimately, we demonstrated the highest gains of any of the district schools. In addition, the components adopted by the district actualized student achievement when implemented with integrity.

Lonnie? He graduated with a placement in a general education classroom. As for me, the practices that I helped the staff and school to implement led to the award of a *Gaining Early Awareness and Readiness for Undergraduate Programs* (GEAR UP) grant. This discretionary grant program was designed to increase the number of low-income students prepared to enter and succeed in post-secondary education. GEAR UP provided (and still provides) six-year or seven-year grants to states and partnerships, which allow them to provide services to high-poverty middle and high schools. The program grantees serve an entire cohort of students from the seventh grade to high school. The funds received provided college scholarships to low-income students.

Needless to say, the year ended on a good note, and the State Secretary of Education did not have to follow through on the

"Reconstitution" of the school. God was faithful throughout the process as I worked alongside staff and the community to move the school from "Reconstitution" to "Good Standing." When I think about this experience, I am reminded that practices that incorporate unbelief in achievement can destroy an institution. However, the exemplary practices—those backed by data, confidence and faith, will empower and effect positive change.

LEADERSHIP CORNER

What practices have you implemented to ensure effective leadership? What practices should you employ? No matter your role in the educational system, your practices will expose your belief system. It's easy for us to keep doing what we have always done. It's easy for us to turn a blind eye to a failing system. The reality is that change takes a concerted effort, but change is necessary. So, I challenge you to think critically about what you have been doing as a teacher, assistant principal, principal, assistant superintendent, or even superintendent. What practices can you implement to move your students from "Reconstitution" to "Good Standing"? Whatever practice you choose, ensure they are undergirded with the efficacy philosophy and the capacity to mobilize effective effort and deliver results.

Leadership Lesson: Confidence, faith, commitment, focus, strategy, and effort are effective practices that lead to achievement.

Scripture Support: *"Listen carefully, I am about to do a new thing, now it will spring forth; will you not be aware of it? I will even put a road in the wilderness, rivers in the desert. (Isaiah 43:19 AMP)*

12

STOP CANCELING THEIR FUTURE: PRACTICES TO AVOID

We are educational leaders, but we all operate in multiple roles. We are aunts, uncles, cousins, sisters, brothers, friends, grandparents, mothers, and fathers. For those of us who are parents, we know what it's like to show up for our students, and we pray that as we do our best to serve, others will show up for our children. However, that's not always the case.

As a mother, I want the best for my children. I want the best experiences, education, and educators to help them succeed in life. Looking back, I can honestly say that each child has had some great educational influences, but there is one unfavorable incident that left an indelible mark on my mind—one that I placed on my "never do" list as I embarked on my educational leadership journey.

My daughter was failing math. She received a "D" and had to attend summer school. This turned out to be a blessing. Mr. Bentley, the summer school teacher, believed in my daughter. He affirmed and encouraged her, while giving her the tools to succeed. With time, effort, and practice, Shelley began to excel in math. She did so well that she began tutoring other students in the summer class and was recommended for honors math the following semester.

She was excited! She could not wait for the new school year to begin. She worked hard and beamed at the thought of being a math honor student. But that excitement quickly faded when, on the first day of school, her former math teacher stopped her from entering the honors class.

"Mom!" I could hear the hysteria in her voice. She continued, "Mr. Rogers said I didn't belong in the honors math class!"

My response was, "Sit in the office. I'm coming!"

I was angry, to say the least! I left work, went home, and although I could hear my mother's voice in the back of my mind saying, "Good girls don't wear black leather," I grabbed my black leather pants and jacket from the back of my closet, and I was ready to go! All I needed was a Harley-Davidson to finish the look! But seriously, at that moment, I didn't care about being *good*, or even *bad*...I just wanted some answers.

"I'd like to speak with Principal Walters, please."

"He's not available," The secretary said.

"Oh okay. No problem. I will just go to the central office to see an Assistant Superintendent or the Superintendent."

"Uhm, one second, Mrs. Wortham. Let me check again."

It's funny how the mention of the central office changed everything. When the principal finally emerged from his office, I had one question for him: "Who gave Mr. Rogers the right to cancel my daughter's future?"

Eyes wide opened, he did not know what to say. I continued, "No one has the right to bring my child low and destroy her capacity to believe that through hard work she could excel in math or anything!"

"No one, Mrs. Wortham! No one has that right. I'm so sorry. I will take care of it."

Ultimately, Mr. Rogers received a reprimand, and eventually, my daughter excelled not only in math, but also in life. She graduated from the University of Maryland Eastern Shore (HBCU) with a Bachelor's in Science, received an M.A. from Morgan State University, and achieved a Doctorate in Science Education. She even became an author who uplifts and inspires children and families with her book, *Family Science Nights*.

I have carried this story and experience with me throughout my career. It is a constant reminder of practices to avoid. It's a reminder to be cognizant of the ways we, as educational leaders, can build or break a child's confidence. It's a reminder to show up for the students, the way I wanted educators to show up for my children. It is a reminder to avoid anything that could possibly cancel their future. For me, that meant a constant evaluation of staff's mindsets, behaviors, and language. What do they think about the students? How do they interact with them? What overt and covert messages are they sending the students through their actions and words? This experience is a constant reminder to do my part to ensure all staff are equipped to set the atmosphere for learning and success.

LEADERSHIP CORNER

Take a moment to do an honest assessment of yourself. Looking at your career, would anyone be able to accuse you of attempting to cancel a student's future? If so, don't be too hard on yourself. Being honest with yourself is the first step to transformation. How can you change the narrative? How can you empower and not deflate dreams? How can you build and not break a child's confidence in themselves and their capacity to learn?

Leadership Lesson: Build them up; don't break them down.

Scripture Support: *"Let no corrupting talk come out of your mouths, but only such as is good for building up, as fits the occasion, that it may give grace to those who hear."* (Ephesians 4:29 ESV)

13

PRACTICAL CHANGES THAT SHIFT THE ATMOSPHERE

"I had a dream that you were the principal of the boiler room," said Mrs. Lee, the principal.

Oh, okay, I thought.

"From now on, you will not be in the classrooms. I'm assigning you to morning entry, cafeteria periods, and dismissal, and you'll have to handle the discipline of 700 students." As an assistant principal, my job was to support the principal's work and initiatives for the school's overall success. I understood the importance of unity among administrators and how necessary it was to avoid friction, as it hinders the development of a positive organizational culture. So, I gladly accepted my non-academic assignment,

"Okay, I got it, Mrs. Lee."

One of the most successful women that I admire is Oprah Winfrey. I admire so many things about her, but one of the traits I like the most is her capacity to connect with her audience. She has a remarkable capacity to create trust as she walks with a microphone in hand, sharing space and talking with others. She mastered the power of her voice, connections, and relationships, and I wanted to emulate her. Although the assignment appeared non-academic,

I knew I needed to build relationships to set the atmosphere for learning. Students can only learn from people they like and trust. So, I had a vision of how to master the tasks at hand.

In setting the atmosphere, one must gain control mentally, physically, and spiritually. When peace is present, one can think creatively. One of the first shifts I made was the establishment of the *Morning Fellowship*. During my time with the children, I learned each child's name. Knowing someone's name is one of the most powerful tools in leadership. Knowing someone's name means "you care and believe in their success." During the Morning Fellowship, I mastered the "walk and talk" for maximum communication and collaboration. Each morning, as the students entered the building, they would line up on both sides of the round hallway. They couldn't see me simultaneously, but they all heard my voice. I would speak affirmations, encouragement, and reassurance as they stood there. No matter what they had experienced at home or what may have troubled them the night before, they knew they were now in an atmosphere of positive promise, and none felt left out. Every day, I witnessed students getting to school on time and even early to participate in the *Morning Fellowship*. Throughout the day, I saw students discussing the fellowship. It was their vitamin and a time for social-emotional experiences. *Morning Fellowship* became the transformative practice that set the atmosphere for the day.

My second initiative was the *Finer Diner* for the lunch periods. Before I became an assistant principal, I served as the first Coordinator for Success for All at Johns Hopkins University and visited the school frequently. I knew about the behavior in the cafeteria. Now, with the management of the lunch periods assigned to me, I had to make a shift in the atmosphere. The first shift was renaming the cafeteria to "The Finer Diner." I thought, "One would never misbehave in a fine dining establishment!" A pivotal part of the initiative was recruiting parents to serve as *Finer Diner Moms and Dads*. In my Oprah Winfrey voice, I went from parent to parent, initiating them for service, "And you get an apron! And you get a chef's hat!" With the *Finer Diner Moms and Dads* in place, students placed their napkins in their laps with the knife and fork set accordingly in preparation to go to a restaurant for lunch and put their practices into action. There were no "diner discrepancies!" Our fine dining lunchroom became a space for breaking bread together, sharing, and dialogue. Rich conversations took place with each student individually and collectively. With a cordless microphone in hand, we harnessed the power of walking and talking, sharing space that created trust. The students and parents discussed everything from school progress to local and international issues, and much like Oprah, there were even moments of gift-giving. We enjoyed a fine dining experience and worked together daily to maintain an atmosphere where all students felt seen and heard.

I may have been assigned a non-academic role, but I learned the importance of showing up excellently no matter where I am planted. I learned the value of implementing small, practical changes that yield significant differences in students' lives and the school's success. What was perceived as a "non-academic" assignment became the key to success. Being visible among the student body and communicating authentically, allowed me to build relationships with students. And here's the best part: I witnessed the power of these practices upon becoming a Superintendent, and *Finer Diner* establishments became the norm nationwide. To God be all the glory!

LEADERSHIP CORNER

You may have been assigned to the "boiler room"—to a role that does not fit your expertise—but be at peace with your assignment. Your mental disposition will determine your creative capacity, enabling you to thrive in that position. This is an opportunity for you to tap into your creative mind and implement practices that perhaps no one else has conceived. How can you think about this new role/assignment from a different perspective? How can you use this opportunity to make the children you serve feel valued, worthy, and seen? What practices can you implement in this assignment that will set the atmosphere for current and future success?

Leadership Lesson: Positive thinking births creativity for practical changes.

Scripture Support: *"Finally, brothers and sisters, whatever is true, whatever is noble, whatever is right, whatever is pure, whatever is lovely, whatever is admirable— if anything is excellent or praiseworthy—think about such things." (Philippians 4:8 NIV)*

14

LET THEM SPEAK: STUDENTS' VOICES MATTER

On the first day on the job as the first female African-American superintendent of this district, I brought two things with me…my purse and my faith. I knew I needed everything in my purse, and I needed every bit of my faith. I was ready for the job! On that day, my first assignment was to visit the schools in my district. This allowed me to introduce myself to the faculty and students, get a feel for the school's culture, check out the environment, and hear from the students themselves. This is one of the most important steps for a new superintendent of a district, and I was looking forward to it.

As my cabinet and I visited each school, I asked students, "What can I do to be the best superintendent ever?"

Their responses varied: "Will you provide healthier options for school lunches?"

"How can you guarantee our safety? We want to feel safe when we enter the school grounds."

"What resources will you provide for the immigrant population of the school body, especially for the non-English speaking students and families?"

"How will you develop our creative arts program and after-school opportunities? Will you provide more electives?"

"Will you implement more higher-level courses for those who feel we are not being challenged?"

These children were not afraid to ask hard questions. They asked and kept asking, but here's the thing…they never asked for my credentials. They only wanted to see if I cared. Caring meant allowing them to speak their truth, ask their questions, and let their voices be heard.

That day, students gave me my marching orders. I listened intently to their concerns, and the mission for my assignment became clear—I would be the students' superintendent. I was energized! The commitment to the students felt intense, with a sense of urgency. Although I went through multiple interviews before being hired, this on-the-job student interview placed my energy in a different direction. Their voices were clear as they spoke up and advocated for their fellow students.

Not long after my first day, I received information that a community organization encouraged students to conduct a protest and walk out during the day. The protest was centered around conditions in the schools before my arrival. The students shared the demands confidentially. Their letter read as follows:

> Hi Dr. Wortham,
>
> Here's what's happening and some points made by the students that I spoke with:
>
> Students met several times over the past three weeks

with several community members. Students have a planned walkout from the high schools. They will leave at the beginning of the sixth period this Friday. All the students will walk to the park, and all the community adults will meet the students there. All the students and adults will then walk to the administration building for a protest. We were able to get permits for the rally. A student leader is in charge, and they will start giving directions tomorrow on social media. I sent you the list of demands.

Here are the demands:

1. *Renovate the schools.*
2. *Build new bleachers.*
3. *Provide sufficient ESL programs.*
4. *A prolonged conversation with the Board.*
5. *No consequences for either walking out or supporting the said walkout.*

Oh, okay, I thought. *Lord, I trust you to give me the wisdom to advocate for the children while dealing with the community's opposition. Let the work begin!*

Having formed relationships with student leaders, I went to each high school to meet with them. We held mini assemblies, during which I informed the students about the progress made in a short time. Students were delighted to know that the new superintendent did not dismiss their concerns, but their voices were heard. They were energized! They even wanted to ride the district bus to the next high school to strategize with the student leaders there. I will never forget how the student leaders led the assembly the day I called the student population to the auditorium. It was student advocacy at its finest. I stood on the side of the auditorium and listened to their voices as they pleaded their case and stood up for their rights. I stood there beaming at the thought that these children were our future leaders.

So, what happened to the walk-out? Well, that turned into a rally with community support and police escorts to provide safety. However, instead of demands and laments, students spoke of the new hope they witnessed during my meetings with them. And what did I do? I continued to work hard to be the students' superintendent and meet their demands. Eventually, we passed a $58,000,000 bond, which gave us the funds to upgrade the facilities, and to top it off, one of the student leaders was appointed to the Board, without the capacity to vote. Following this incident, we implemented the *Superintendent Student Circle*, which allowed student leaders to meet with me weekly to discuss what they believed we were doing well, what we could improve, and the overall school culture. This all happened because the students spoke up, and their voices were heard.

LEADERSHIP CORNER

While some educational leaders may have considered the students' actions disruptive and even divisive, I considered them powerful. It is so easy to try to stifle their voice and label them as insubordinate, but their voice matters. There is power in their collective voices, and as educational leaders, we must not only allow them to speak, but we must also listen. Listening to children's voices requires humility and an understanding that their input is an integral component of school development and growth. Although the above narrative initiated the *Superintendent Student Circle*, it is still a critical practice that I use in my current district. I've even implemented several superintendent circles throughout my career that provide a space for dialogue between me and students, teachers, and the community. So, how have you allowed them to speak? Are you listening… really listening? What forum have you provided so that their voices can be heard? Or have you been attempting to stifle their voice?

Leadership Lesson: You cannot effectively serve a community that you have not heard from. Success will be difficult without their voice. Let them speak.

Scripture Support: *"I have no greater joy than to hear that my children are walking in the truth." (3 John 1:4 ESV)*

15

ADMINISTER A VACCINE OF VISION AND A BOOSTER OF BELIEF

I had always been careful about my health. I made sure to get my yearly physicals, vaccines, and all the check-ups necessary to ensure that I had optimal health. While there had been some concerns here and there, ones that required watch care for a few years, and several biopsies throughout the years, a cancer diagnosis was far from my mind. I was diligent about my health and made sure to do my personal checks, during which I never felt a lump. However, following one of my yearly diagnostic mammograms, I was diagnosed with stage 0 breast cancer. I was shocked, and after coming to terms with the diagnosis, I knew what I needed to do. I needed to approach this circumstance with faith, much like I had done with any other adverse situation or challenge I have had to face throughout my life. So, after much prayer, a lumpectomy, eight weeks of radiation, and five years of taking Tamoxifen, I was declared cancer-free. Today, I am a 22-year breast cancer survivor.

Since dealing with this life-altering experience with cancer, I've become more of an advocate for the equitable access and distribution of health resources for minority communities. As a woman of color,

I understand the importance of shining a light on health disparities not only during the month of April when we celebrate National Minority Health, but throughout the year. As a member of the minority community, I believe we must become credible messengers and market information that affects communities of color. We must shine a light on preventable differences in opportunities to achieve optimal health for disadvantaged people due to their social or economic status, geographic location, and/or environment. In addition, we must be dedicated to improving health outcomes for racial and ethnic minority groups. But here's the thing, I also believe that as educational leaders, we too must shine a light on educational health disparities within our school systems. These systems and practices sustain inequality in access to high-quality education, resulting in inferior reading and math proficiency, lower high school graduation rates, and hindrances to college acceptance.

The COVID-19 pandemic uncovered much of what was hidden under the proverbial educational hood of systems that have placed minority children at a disadvantage. Suddenly, there were discussions about which districts qualified for vaccines and when; who met the CDC guidelines for childcare who should be masked and who was exempt, and who had access to technology and Wi-Fi and who did not. Suddenly, we could all see clearly how minority children were disproportionately affected by the lack of resources in our communities. But this health pandemic uncovered so much more. It uncovered an academic pandemic of low expectations—a silent killer of dreams, desires, and destiny.

As we head towards the end of this pandemic, there has been talk about "learning loss" due to COVID-19, but as one who has served as an educational leader for many years, I will say that this loss has always been there. There has been a loss of confidence in our children. Based on demographics and zip codes, low expectations have been the norm for children of color. Policies and practices have translated to "we don't believe in you," therefore, they don't believe in themselves. We have neglected to provide them with the necessary resources to thrive; therefore, many have adopted a belief in mediocrity. So, how do we change this narrative? As educational leaders, we must strive for educational health equity—access to and distribution of resources regardless of race, gender, or zip code. We want to educate the whole child and guarantee all students are healthy, safe, supported, engaged, and challenged. As educational leaders, we must administer a vaccine of vision and a booster of belief to the children we serve.

A vaccine of vision and a booster of belief require us to evaluate how we see them as teachers, administrators, principals, superintendents, and all who are in contact with our youth. Do you believe in your students? Do they know that you believe in them? Can you look beyond where they are and see them in a bright, successful future, and have you shared that vision with them? "Out of the abundance of the heart, the mouth speaks" (Matthew 12:34). What has been rooted in your heart that you are now saying to them? Adapt practices that infuse vision and bolster belief. Speak life over them and their families.

Set the atmosphere for success by implementing programs that allow each child to feel seen, affirmed, and welcomed. Encourage youth to have and maintain a growth mindset. When we do our best to administer a vaccine of vision and a booster of belief, we will create healthy environments for children to glow and grow.

LEADERSHIP CORNER

We never know the challenges we will have to face in life. In my personal life, I had to face breast cancer, and so I advocate for early detection. In my career as an educational leader, I also advocate for the early detection of unhealthy systems and practices that adversely affect our children. How do you see yourself administering a vaccine of vision and a booster of belief?

Leadership Lesson: Early detection and clear diagnosis prevent an academic pandemic.

Scripture Support: *"Where there is no vision, the people perish; but happy is he who keeps the teaching." (Proverbs 29:18 MEV)*

PART 4

PROTOCOLS THAT SET
THE ATMOSPHERE

The difference between 'practices' and 'protocols' is that practices are fluid, suggestive, and subjective. Protocols, on the other hand, are foundational standards by which educational leaders build sustainable, healthy, successful environments where all thrive. The following narratives present protocols that have proven to be necessary and pivotal to setting the atmosphere.

16

IT TAKES A VILLAGE

"You're a liar!" These were the words from a parent as I concluded my first high school back-to-school night as a superintendent on the East Coast. I was new to the district, and I was prepared for everything that I knew would come my way that evening. I was not upset; I understood. I understood the frustration of the parents and community. They were concerned about lagging academic results, well-publicized student behavioral matters, and overall low-performing schools, and they needed answers. They wanted a change, and I was up for the challenge.

One of the first things I knew I needed to do was gather my village—influencers, leaders, and stakeholders who were committed to the success of the schools. I met with the President of the Council along with several clergy, and together we established a listening tour to build relationships and gauge the community's pulse. We knocked on doors, distributed fliers, and held "porch talks" about forthcoming school changes. Within the first thirty days of my superintendency, I met with more than 400 community members, board members, staff, and students, either individually or in small groups, all of whom were essential members of the village.

It was particularly important for me to ensure synergy between two critical members of the village, the staff, and students. One way we did this was to use the district's mission statement to provide a common language and build relationships among the parties. In addition, central office staff members, including facilities and food service staff, spent the first hour of their day helping with busing, morning entry, the breakfast program, and institutionalizing the new dress code protocol. Their presence in the schools made a difference.

Our efforts to empower and equip key village members continued with a book study of *Failure is Not an Option by Alan Blankstein*. All district staff and the nine-member board participated in the reading and implementation of the book's six principles. Principals and teacher leaders used the principles to (1) create a shared mission, vision, values, and goals; (2) ensure achievement for all students: systems for prevention and intervention; (3) create collaborative teaming focused on teaching and learning; (4) use data to guide decision-making and continuous improvement; (5) gain active engagement from family and community; and (6) build sustainable leadership capacity.

The partner, parent, student, and mentor members of the village needed to also play a significant role in the success of the district. They all had to participate in a commitment ceremony. During this event, high school seniors would pledge to attain seven criteria for "walking the stage." These *Essential 7* were: Take the SAT or ACT, complete college applications, attend classes regularly with positive behavior, complete the State Prep (a state remediation course), complete the service-learning project, earn a passing GPA, and complete the graduation project. In addition, the state university sponsored an on-site college office at the high school and assigned a college adviser to support this initiative. The college advisor worked with the school's guidance counselor, teacher mentors, and the principal to coach students in meeting the *Essential 7*.

One year following that first back-to-school night event, we made considerable progress in several areas. Notably, we advanced the college-going rate significantly, with seniors being accepted to thirteen different colleges, and the remaining students having post-secondary plans. Two years later, high school attendance went from 87 percent to 89 percent. The number of suspensions decreased from 225 to 146. *The high school's graduation rate increased to 92 percent,* and all 80 graduates had acceptances to 64 schools. The average SAT score improved from 794 to 820. In addition, according to the State Assessment System (a measure of progress and growth), middle school 8th graders scored in the top 20% for growth in reading, math, and writing during the school year. Students in the 11th grade were in the top quintile for growth in writing. But my greatest joy was having a 100 percent college-going rate during my final year as the superintendent of that school district. This all took place two years after being accused of being a "liar" and the parent not believing that all the students could graduate.

LEADERSHIP CORNER

Your village matters to your success as an educational leader. They are key individuals within your organization and within the community. These individuals may not be able to invest a great deal of time, but what they have to offer is valuable to your mission and vision. Have you identified the members of your village? Who are your influencers, community leaders, and stakeholders who will work alongside you for future success?

Leadership Lesson: It takes a village to educate the future.

Scripture Support: *"Where there is no counsel, the people fall; but in the multitude of counselors there is safety."* *(Proverbs 11:14 NKJV)*

17

PROFICIENCY PARTNERS

"**D**r. Wortham, we need to talk with you. We don't know what to do. The students aren't reading at their grade level, and their scores are low! What should we do?" Two teachers approached me with panic in their voices. At first, I had no idea how to respond to them, but I took a deep breath and responded,

"Teach them on grade level and then create differentiated instructional groups based on data."

"Oh! That sounds good! Thanks, Dr. Wortham!"

As they left my office, I saw a renewed confidence and excitement on these teachers' faces. They were looking for a solution, and my suggestion, albeit in my attempt to dismiss them, was the answer they needed. What I didn't know at the time was how they would leverage collegial support to enhance student achievement.

Along with another teacher, these teachers created a powerful triad of proficiency partners. Together, their goal was proficiency for all the students they served. They created a professional network that was second to none—one that served as a model for the entire building and focused on accountability, effective strategies for learning, and instruction. The teachers became proficient in their practice as a result of their partnership. The time they spent together talking about their craft and adding to their own individual and collective repertoire paid off in the achievements of their students.

To achieve our goals and make a difference in the lives of our students, we need the support and collaboration of others. We need proficiency partners—colleagues with a shared belief, passion, and commitment. Together, these leaders embrace a silent oath that they will make a difference. By working together and supporting each other, they are able to overcome obstacles and achieve success. Proficiency partners may be a team of two, or a group of three, four, five, or more educational leaders coming together on a consistent basis to provide feedback, share ideas, and forge a path towards collective success. As such, it is important that as we think about whom to partner with on this proficiency journey, we consider the following:

1. *Does each member share the same belief about their capability, and the capability of the students they serve?* It is crucial to determine the beliefs teachers have about their own capabilities and how students learn. Do they have a fixed mindset, or a growth mindset? Every teacher is bound to have their own beliefs and understanding of what constitutes best practices. Beliefs are deeply rooted in both personal experience and culture. They are action agendas for behaviors; they guide a person's intentions in setting an academically-sound atmosphere.

2. *Are all proficiency partners committed to the development of their own proficiency?* In other words, do they all embody a growth mindset, which fuels their efforts to keep learning, improving their skills, and a devotion to professional development? We cannot expect students to be proficient when we are not proficient. Efficacious members are crucial to setting a learning atmosphere.

3. *Are all proficiency members willing to play a supportive role in the learning community?* This means they are partners of encouragement, working together to assess progress toward goals, identifying obstacles, and delineating a plan to overcome barriers.

LEADERSHIP CORNER

Encouraging staff and teacher leaders to form proficiency partnerships is vital to school improvement and has proven to be a protocol that has enabled me to set the atmosphere within the districts I have served. Leaders must set the atmosphere for students to succeed through commitment and effort. Teachers must manage students' development so they may acquire the self-confidence that will enable them to have a quality life. Proficiency partnerships empower educational leaders to show up and be their best, give their best, and do their best.

Leadership Lesson: When we work together, we are stronger and more effective.

Scripture Support: *"Two are better than one, because they have a good return for their labor: If either of them falls down, one can help the other up. But pity anyone who falls and has no one to help them up." Ecclesiastes 4:9-10 (NIV)*

18

DEVELOPING A DATA-DRIVEN DISTRICT

As the new superintendent of a large district, I needed up-to-date data on student achievement. I needed to understand why the State Department rated the district as "School Improvement" and students were not achieving at higher levels. I took this position in November, so I needed to see the data from the first quarterly assessment, as well as the historical data. So, I did what any new superintendent would do, I asked the staff to present me with their quarterly reports.

Their response was, "Uhm, Dr. Wortham, we don't have any quarterly reports."

I responded, "Well, how do you know how the students perform?"

I heard crickets. Then, a brave soul replied, "Teacher judgment."

Oh wow! That's interesting! How could this be? I thought.

Relying solely on teachers' judgment does not provide valid and reliable data. Not having quarterly assessments is one reason there's a gap in student achievement between the district and the state. It was obvious that this district's practices were not in alignment with state standards, and we were in a data-driven deficit.

One of the first things I needed to do was get an audit. I immediately contacted a well-known assessment company to conduct an audit of the district's assessment practices. The audit revealed teacher behavior and performance, areas where students were failing, and the overall practices and protocols that have resulted in the district's underachievement. With information on hand, I now had what I needed to make informed decisions. The data was analyzed, and after some negotiations with the board, I got a proposal approved that would allow the district to adopt a quarterly assessment process that aligned with the state's standards. This assessment process came at a hefty price of $110,000, but it was worth it, since it had a 95 percent accuracy rate compared to the standard state assessment. When administered quarterly, it provided us with a clear picture of the district's strengths, as well as areas in need of improvement. The assessment also predicted performance and enabled us to allocate resources to support student success.

The district was now a data-driven district. No longer were we relying on "teacher judgment." We now had an assessment process with valid, reliable data that would deliver achievement and growth measures on time, and with proper instructions. All educational leaders and staff were trained to use the new data for screening, progress monitoring, and instructional planning. The district was empowered by information, and each principal gained tremendous confidence in their capacity to lead. In addition, teachers created Data Walls and Data Conferences, which provided spaces for the students to articulate the steps they were taking to grow and achieve. Bulletin boards became *instructional learning boards* that informed students of the learning process and progress. This included the learning target, rubric, and state standard.

A data-driven district meant that all were enlightened, equipped, and empowered to learn and grow. Data undergirded all our schools' initiatives and allowed us to set and reset the atmosphere for student success. Data helped us create a vision for the future—one that was sustainable and achievable. This district was transformed from a data-deficit district to a data-abundance district. Our new systems and protocols worked so well that by the end of two years, one school became an International Baccalaureate school, and all twelve K–8 schools were no longer rated as "school improvement," but all were in "good standing," thanks to data.

LEADERSHIP CORNER:

Without data, we have no real system in place to evaluate where we are and where we need to go. Data is a vital tool for all educational leaders. Data informs our teaching strategies. Data informs our practices and protocols. Data helps us to create a vision and plans that guarantee the success of all students. What protocols are in place that allow you to collect accurate data? How can you use this data to inform your decisions?

Leadership Lessons: Data informs the steps to success.

Scripture: *"So we fix our eyes not on what is seen, but on what is unseen, since what is seen is temporary, but what is unseen is eternal." (2 Corinthians 4:18 NIV)*

19

SEE SOMETHING, SAY SOMETHING: THE PARENT-TEACHER CONNECTION

"A smiley face again?!" My son beamed with a sense of achievement as he handed me another one of his school assignments with a smiling face indicating his progress.

"I'm so proud of you, son! Keep up the good work!" As he walked off with a huge grin on his face, I would smile and think, "Well, the apple doesn't fall far from the tree!" Daily he handed me that paper with a smiley face, and daily he beamed, and I affirmed. He was doing well, and I was proud of his progress. So when it was time for his school's PTA meeting, my husband and I were excited to hear from his teachers about how great our son was doing.

As my husband and I entered the classroom, we noticed our son's name on the board with an asterisk next to it. We both smiled and thought, *Wow! He must be doing better than we thought! That must mean, "Well, well done!"* We were filled with even more joy and excitement. We were eager and waited anxiously for our turn with his second-grade teacher.

"Good evening, Mr. and Mrs. Wortham. So glad to meet you and happy you both were able to make it." We sat down in anticipation of the good news. Mrs. Smith continued, "There are some things I want to discuss with you. Your son's name is on the board because, while your son is doing well academically, he talks entirely too much in class."

Stunned, I responded, "What?! I know my son is highly skilled in the art of communication, so what does that mean? He brought home a *smiley face* each day. I thought all was going well?!"

"I'm not sure what you are talking about, Mrs. Wortham. I only gave him one smiley face, and all the other days, he received a worm."

I started putting all the pieces together and realized that each day my son handed me that recycled "smiley face," he walked away with a sense of accomplishment because he was successful in his quest to cover up his behavior in class.

We were in disbelief. At that moment, it all made sense to not only me and my husband, but also to Mrs. Smith. She exclaimed, "I wondered why I didn't hear from you all." But here's the thing...we were wondering the same thing about her! Why didn't she contact us?!

Chet was on punishment for 180 days, and following that incident, we never had to reprimand him again. Thank God! However, that experience reminded me of the importance of the educator's voice. As educational leaders, we spend hours after hours with children and oftentimes experience them differently from their parents. In other words, what happens at school may not be what happens at home, and when we see something, we must say something. Setting the atmosphere for success requires a good parent-teacher connection—one that is consistent, open, and honest.

Now, as educators, we must be consistent in our attempt to make the connection with parents. It is our responsibility to keep parents abreast of their children's progress. It is our responsibility to build trust—one that lets parents know that you have the child's best interest at heart. If you see something, say something. If a child seems consistently weary, lethargic, or inattentive, then say something. If a child just does not seem to be improving, and no matter how many "worms" you give them, and the parents have not contacted you, then you contact them. If a child seems depressed and isolated, say something.

Good leaders are proactive and not reactive. Good educational leaders are in constant dialogue with parents—informing them of progress and areas in need of improvement. Good educational leaders understand that parents are pivotal to their efforts in setting the atmosphere. However, here's another thing I discovered during that "smiley face dilemma"…it's not that some children "speak too much" because of a need to be disruptive, but because they have been taught the value of their voice. As educational leaders, we must empower young voices from all races, nationalities, genders, and religions. Today, Chet is an accomplished financial analyst using his skill in communication to broker deals worth millions of dollars. If you see something, say something.

LEADERSHIP CORNER:

It is so easy to be overwhelmed with all the responsibilities of an educator. I understand. However, building that parent-educator connection is the key to less stress and future success. How can you build or strengthen that connection? Is there anything you have seen that you have not voiced?

Leadership Lesson: See something, say something. Build the connection.

Scripture Support: *"So David shepherded them according to the integrity of his heart; and guided them with his skillful hands." (Psalm 78:72 AMP)*

20

THE FINAL 5—INCREASING THE GRADUATION LEVEL

"The lazy rate" was how I often referred to low graduation rates. I coined the term in reference to the lack of effort by some administrators to identify the root cause of students not meeting graduation requirements. Serving for three years as the Area Academic Officer (Assistant Superintendent) for twenty-four citywide and special needs high schools, I was able to not only have a birds-eye view of the root causes of low academic achievement, but I was also able to narrow in on the critical issues that needed to be fixed. As an educational leader, I learned the art of introspection—of taking a deep look within one's district, acknowledging what's working, while accepting what's broken. This school district was broken, and we needed to accept our role in the dysfunction, roll up our sleeves, and get to work fixing it.

The graduation rate reflects the relationship to, collaboration within, and responsibility of the entire district. A cohesive culture is a visible illustration of staff united with a similar mindset. Every member of the district and community must hold themselves accountable for all students graduating on time. As such, one of the first protocols implemented was the *Find Them, Teach Them, Send Them on Their Way* strategy. We believed there was a sequential correlation between the registration and attendance process (*Find Them*), instruction (*Teach Them*), and continuous support (*Send Them on Their Way*). Monitoring the process and progress of each student from the moment of registration was critical. Staff had to document and articulate the entry and exit of each student with fidelity.

We had to *find them* daily—that was an essential part of our accountability. In addition, we had to value all students and communicate the importance of their presence. The instructional process, *teach them*, was vital for student engagement and the fueling of student attendance. However, collaboration among staff was critical when students were visibly present but disconnected from the learning process. Together staff was tasked with identifying the connection between disengaged students and their mission to know each child by name, making them feel seen and welcomed, and *sending them on their way.*

Another major protocol that was vital to the success of the students and the increase in the graduation rate was the *Final Five*. With this strategy, students had to agree to take the SAT or ACT, have acceptable attendance with good behavior, an acceptable GPA, apply to a college, and complete fifty hours of community service. Upon completion, students were guaranteed that they would walk the stage. To ensure success, each student was assigned a mentor and a counselor. In addition, courses were added, the attendance summary was evaluated, and student data was analyzed. Regular feedback prevented fragmentation, and maintenance of achievement was guaranteed.

A component of the *Final Five* strategy included a commitment ceremony, which was held in October. During this standing-room-only ceremony, parents, mentors, and students recited vows and made a commitment to do their best to make sure that all graduated high school on time. One of the evening's highlights was the moment when each student got to practice walking the stage.

These strategies were successful, and we witnessed student after student walk the graduation stage. *The lazy rate* was no longer an issue for the district because every administrator made a commitment to the district's goal of knowing every child by name. We were committed to each student, holding them accountable while celebrating their determination to succeed, in spite of familial, economic, or social issues and possible deterrents. *The Final Five* was successful then and has proven to be successful thereafter.

LEADERSHIP CORNER

There is a misconception that students drop out in the ninth grade, but my experiences have taught me that that perception is wrong. The reality is that by the second grade, students have made the decision to drop out, or not show up, because they did not master the needed skills to succeed in the third grade. Students need structure, a roadmap to success, encouragement, and accountability. The graduation rate sits in the palm of everyone's hand. What protocols can you begin to put in place to increase your school's graduation rate?

Leadership Lesson: The graduation rate is the responsibility of the entire district, and reflects the power of leaders to cultivate, collaborate, and influence relationships.

Scripture Support*: "As iron sharpens iron, so one person sharpens another." (Proverbs 27:17 NIV)*

21

LEAD BY EXAMPLE

I'm sure you have heard the saying, "You have one chance to make a good impression." Throughout my life, I understood that to mean that first impressions have the power to close doors or open amazing ones. Through appearance, intelligence, and character, we have one chance to present our very best to the world. In fact, from the onset of my career, there has been an emphasis on attire, and a required unwritten dress code among leaders. I didn't need a memo; no one had to tell me, all I had to do was look around the room. As I moved through the ranks of my career, participating in meeting after meeting, gathering after gathering, in district after district, I noticed how each leader possessed a particular style that transcended the district. I gleaned from each, but over time I developed my own sense of style.

This belief in presenting the best forward carried me throughout my career, and so when I found myself saying, "Pull up your pants!," over and over again, day after day, I knew I needed to establish some standards. What do you do when you have a population of young men with their pants hanging down? We lead by example.

As a Superintendent, I rallied the men together and asked

if they would help launch an initiative to shift the culture in the district. The leadership strategy merely asked all men to wear ties. Now, this may sound archaic, but my thought process was, "How can we ever impress upon students the necessity of pulling up their pants, if there are no standards to emulate?" So, the men agreed to wear ties and belts. Instead of shouting the directive, "Pull up your pants!," we coined the phrase, "The higher the pants, the higher the income." The more they heard it, the higher the pants went. These men were visual role models for the male students. As the word spread, the community supported the initiative, with members of various organizations contributing funds to purchase belts for the students. We led by example, and not only did young men begin to carry themselves differently, but so did the young ladies. It was time to set a standard for the girls in my district. Again, I rallied the women, and asked them to adorn themselves in business attire. Instead of saying, "Pull down your skirt!," we shouted, "Ladies, the lower the skirt, the higher the income!" Eventually, skirts became longer, and girls began to embrace a new dress code.

While these initiatives were not academic in nature, they made an impact on both behavior and achievement. Community events like *Guys with Ties and Girls with Pearls* served as rites of passage for the students. Community partners donated ties and pearls, and during the event, they tied the young men's ties and fastened the young women's pearls. Students began to see themselves differently. There was a new sense of pride in oneself—skirts were lower, pants were higher, and heads were lifted. We witnessed a shift in demeanor coupled with a belief in a growth mindset. Students began to believe that they could and would be able to realize their dreams—all because we launched an initiative to lead by example.

How are you leading by example? Students look to us as leaders. If we do not present our best, how can we expect them to present their best? Think about how you can become a role model for the students you serve. Who knows—you may be the only example of excellence in their young lives.

Leadership Lesson: Help them to see themselves in you. Be their reflection.

Scripture Support: *"Let your light shine before men in such a way that they may see your good deeds and moral excellence, and [recognize and honor and] glorify your Father who is in heaven." (Matthew 5:16 AMP)*

22

PROTECTING THE ATMOSPHERE

"There is a sound for the house," said a prominent music director. He further explained that when the sound is cultivated and preserved, it *commands a particular call, response, commitment, and behavior to execute a mellifluous flow, which invites corporate worship that's pleasing to Almighty God.* As he uttered those words, I thought about the necessity for educational leaders to not only set the atmosphere, but to also protect it by identifying, cultivating, and preserving the sound of their district.

Protecting the atmosphere requires intentionality to create the synergy needed to foster a culture of excellence. When the atmosphere is set, the tone and/or mood of a classroom, school, or district is engaging, exciting, and inviting. These spaces then become places where individuals with shared beliefs desire to work together, even above and beyond contractual confines.

Throughout my career, I've witnessed firsthand the harmful effects when the atmosphere isn't protected. An unprotected atmosphere often results in chaos, toxicity, low-staff morale, high student suspensions, low attendance among staff and students, a high staff turnover, and low academic achievement. In this atmosphere, there is no collaboration, synergy, and/or commitment. However, when the atmosphere is protected, staff, students, and the community flourish and thrive. To protect the atmosphere, we must:

1. **Protect the Peace:** This means that everyone should be on one accord. All educational stakeholders (including, but not limited, to teachers, administrators, students, parents, community leaders, boards of education, clericals, security, and facility staff), no matter their role or capacity, must embrace a common mission and vision. As educational leaders, we must ensure that these precepts are clearly articulated and modeled for all. Protecting the peace requires leaders to be astute—always assessing the atmosphere, which enables them to encourage systemic positive attitudes and beliefs, while discouraging demeaning behaviors.

2. **Protect the Place:** This means that we are visible and constantly monitoring the culture—monitoring the way we do business. When leaders are present throughout the building, entering classrooms, orchestrating, and talking about teaching and learning, they are able to build relationships and confirm adherence to the mission and vision. Leaders must embrace the "3-B Strategy." The only reasons principals or superintendents should be in their office and *not* in the classrooms are: "Bullets" (a threat or weapons on campus), "Blood" (a medical emergency), or "Boss" (an authority figure). As educational leaders, our

presence matters.

3. **Protect Proficiency:** This requires aligning expectations and maintaining relevant data that, in turn, allows leaders to be explicit about student and staff achievement. Proficiency is then protected because there is transparency and accountability.

Protecting the atmosphere for achievement and excellence must be an institutionalized protocol. We must fight to protect the atmosphere that we have worked so hard to create. The success of future generations is at stake, so do not run from the fight, but engage, strategize, and win the battle to set and protect the atmosphere.

LEADERSHIP CORNER:

How are you protecting the atmosphere in the classroom, school, and/or district? The atmosphere must be set and protected for the success of all. Protecting the peace, place, and proficiency is the means by which we protect the atmosphere.

Leadership Lesson: A breach in the atmosphere must be noticed, fixed, and protected.

Scripture Support: *"Let us therefore make every effort to do what leads to peace and to mutual edification."* *(Romans 14:19 NIV)*

PART 5

MOVING TO THE NEXT LEVEL

God has called everyone to greater. This means you can't get stuck at your current level. However, as you move up the ladder of success to your "next," there are some essentials that you must take with you on the journey. In the following narratives, I've provided guidance based on my personal experiences to help you navigate your journey on the leadership ladder.

23

THE FIT CHECKLIST

"Sister Deborah, stand up. God has called you to be a superintendent." This was a prophetic declaration from the bishop, spoken directly to me during a Sunday morning worship service. What the bishop did not know at the time was that I had applied to various districts and was expecting God to move on my behalf. Three times he declared those words to me, and each time he spoke, I praised God for confirming what I felt deep within. His words were confirmation that kingdom connections were being made. I believed that God had more in store for me.

This bishop said, "Sister Deborah, words are more for creation than communication," and with that, I knew that my next level was in the office of Superintendency.

I held on to the bishop's words of confirmation as I continued working as a consultant and educational leader, applying for superintendent positions, and waiting on God. One day, I had the opportunity to be a keynote speaker for a district out of state. Following my presentation, instead of taking me directly to the train station, as was the norm, my hosts drove me around the district, showing me one school after another.

"And this is ABC Academy."

"Oh, that's nice. But I really need to head to the station to catch my train."

They responded, "Oh of course, but we really think that you would be a great fit for this district." *You do?!* I thought. "We really think you would be great as our next superintendent."

I had no words. I did not confirm or deny it. But deep down, I didn't think that this was it.

I finally made it back home and the next day, my Chief of Staff approached me. "So, you are interviewing for the position of Superintendent?!"

"No, I am not." He went on to let me know that the district I had visited had called and informed him that they wanted me to be their next superintendent. "I don't think that's for me," I responded.

"Go for the interview and just let them know that you are not interested."

So, I did. While I knew this district was not the place for me, what I gained was experience in interviewing. This interview gave me a window into what to expect, but it also confirmed that there has to be a synergistic fit between the superintendent and the district. For me, the fit was and still is inclusive of location, demographics, performance, personal skill set, experience, vision, passion for the work, salary, and sense of community. Since all my fit components were not aligned, I had the confidence to walk away from a seemingly great opportunity.

I kept working, believing God, and trusting that when one door closes, God will open another. And another indeed was opened…but was this God? After applying and interviewing for a superintendent position in my hometown (which is what I yearned for), I was offered the job. This was a wealthy district, close to my mother and sister, and from the outside, everything about it seemed like it would be right for me, but I knew I needed to check the alignment, so I pulled out my *Fit Checklist:*

- ✓ Location – Fit (I'd have to relocate, but hubby and I would make it work)
- ✓ Demographics – Fit
- ✓ Performance of District – Fit (High performing)
- ✓ Personal skill-set – Fit
- ✓ Experience – Fit
- ✓ Vision – Fit
- ✗ Passion for the work – Not Preferable
- ✓ Salary – Fit
- ✓ Sense of Community – Fit

All the indicators were a fit except one, which, in my opinion, is the most critical factor. Having a passion for the work supersedes everything else. Getting up each morning knowing you are not passionate about the job will negatively impact your confidence, effort, and achievement. So, what did I do? I asked the board to wait while I decided if I would accept other offers (not good advice). They agreed.

I ultimately turned down the position in the wealthy district and accepted an offer that was fully aligned with my *fit checklist*. This position paid half the salary of the other, was located one hour away from where I lived, was ranked #498 (from the bottom) out of 500 districts in that state, and here's the best part...I was passionate about the work! This was my next-level fit!

LEADERSHIP CORNER

You are destined for more. God has more in store for you. Doors will open, but I encourage you to check the *Fit List*. Does everything align? Is this your right fit? Are you right for that school, for that district, or for that position? When we attempt to move to the next level in our careers as educational leaders, we must take inventory of every opportunity that comes our way. It may look good, but is it your fit?

Leadership Lesson: Check the fit checklist now, so you won't have to fight or flee afterwards.

Scripture Support: *"Commit your works to the Lord [submit and trust them to Him], and your plans will succeed [if you respond to His will and guidance]" (Proverbs 16:3 AMP).*

24

NEVER SAY NEVER

"If you ever come to New York, we will take good care of you. There's ministry in New York for you!" These were Rev. Dr. Floyd Flake's words to my husband and me during a T.D. Jakes Cruise many years ago. It was there that we met the Rev. Drs. Floyd and Elaine Flake.

So, what was our response to Dr. Flake's gracious comment? Laughter—Chester and I laughed because we knew we would never move to New York...or so we thought.

While New York was never on my list of states to serve in the capacity of superintendent, I was always drawn to districts with "special" or "unique" circumstances. So, following my assignment in a Pennsylvania district, I felt the urge to apply to a unique district in New York. What was so "unique" or special about this district? Well, for the previous twelve years, the district was taken over by the New York State Education Department. For twelve years, the district was run by a state-appointed monitor and a state-appointed superintendent, both of whom reported to the Commissioner of Education. This was because, for twelve years, the district was fiscally and academically struggling. But, I knew this was where I wanted to serve.

I thought I would never move to New York, but being led by God, I became the first locally appointed superintendent of that district in twelve years. I remember the ribbon-cutting ceremony like it was yesterday. Commissioner John King said to the audience, "I'm placing this district in the hands of the superintendent, Dr. Deborah L. Wortham."

I was delighted to serve and ready for the challenge. In addition, the President of the board, Mr. Robert Summerville, was a tremendous *father figure* to me. Every Wednesday, we would meet for hours, and he would say, "Don't let me die without seeing this district restored to "good standing."

"I promise to do my best, Mr. Summerville." I didn't want to disappoint, and I knew there was work to do.

The board, staff, community, and students worked feverishly to set the atmosphere for success. We established the district's new mission, vision, values, and goals. Together, we created multiple systems for governing, teaching, and learning with integrity, which led to districtwide achievement. Two and a half years after the ribbon-cutting ceremony, I received a letter from the New York State Education Department stating that the district would receive reauthorization in January with a rating of "Good Standing." I kept my promise, and Mr. Summerville was elated. He kept the faith, finished his course, and passed away on May 21st of that year.

I was now invested in the success of New York State's districts. The state I once thought I would never live in or serve was now my home. Following the success of that district, I accepted another position to serve as Superintendent of a larger New York district with state-appointed monitors. Much like the first district, we worked feverishly to set the atmosphere, and put into place all the necessary components for success. Within three years, all twelve K-8 schools were rated in "good standing."

I've learned never to say "never." I have learned the importance of relinquishing all control to God, believing that God will order my steps. I've discovered that success is inevitable when we give up on our plans and accept God's plans. New York was not in my plans, but it was in God's plans, and because I was obedient, I was successful. Being recognized as one of the 100 Most Influential Education Leaders in New York and ranking as one of the top 40 out of 100 leaders is evidence of success that was only possible because I said "yes" to being led by God.

Today, I am still serving New York State, the place I once thought I would never serve. My life and walk with God are constant reminders to never say never. Oh, and what about Pastors Floyd and Elaine Flake? Well, they are still taking good care of us in ministry.

LEADERSHIP CORNER:

What have you said "never" to? God has a way of orchestrating our lives, and your next level will be contingent on you succumbing to the leadership of the Spirit. You may have your own plans for your career—where you want to serve, which schools, with whom—but God's plans will always be greater than our plans.

Leadership Lesson: Never say "Never"

Scripture Support: *"A man's mind plans his way [as he journeys through life], but the LORD directs his steps and establishes them." (Proverbs 16:9 AMP)*

25

ORDERED STEPS

Life has taught me that every experience, good, bad, or indifferent, serves a purpose. I believe that although we may not understand the "why" behind some life experiences, there are lessons to be learned, and sometimes, these experiences are preparation for what's to come. I believe that throughout our lives, when we are obedient to the leadership of God's Spirit, we will walk in God's ordered steps.

My admission as one of 50 African Americans to the University of Wisconsin was a divinely ordered step. It was challenging at times but also rewarding. During my time, I learned how to live harmoniously alongside my classmates, understanding and learning about their culture and sharing my culture. I didn't know it then, but that experience was preparation for what was to come.

Years after my time at the University of Wisconsin, I was seated before a nine-member board seeking a Superintendent's position. My time at the University of Wisconsin had prepared me for this moment, and I was ready. With credentials on the table, reputable references, benchmarks of past successes, and mention of my ministerial ordination, I was offered the position. I was that district's first female African-American superintendent, composed of 10,000 students of color and 20,000 students in private schools. At that moment, I was reminded of Romans 8:28 (KJV), "And we know that all things work together for good to them that love God, to them who are the called according to his purpose." My college years prepared me for that interview before that board and the community I wanted to serve.

I remember it like it was yesterday. It was the first community board meeting that would introduce me as the district's new superintendent. As my colleagues and I walked into the board room, I could hear someone gasp and say, "She's Black!" The community showed up—hundreds of people, including children, held up welcome signs and posters demanding a change in the district's policies, practices, and procedures. I stood there, assessed the situation, and charted a course forward.

"I don't want to talk to posters," I said. "I want to talk to people. Please lower your posters." One by one, signs were lowered, eyes were exposed, and I spoke directly to their hearts. At that moment, I was determined not to allow culture or race to separate us, but to be unified as one people with the goal of seeing each child succeed. Following my remarks and inviting the marching band into the meeting, the atmosphere was set. Community members were cheering, hands were clapping (albeit offbeat at times), and all felt heard, encouraged, and hopeful. That moment marked the beginning of my relationship with the community.

As you move up to the next level in your career, know that

all your life experiences will serve you if you have taken the time to glean and apply the skills and lessons learned. Do not discount any experience, no matter how trivial or traumatic it may have been. Those were divinely ordered steps. You are stronger, wiser, knowledgeable, discerning, skillful, empathetic, qualified, and better equipped for your next. As you move forward, trust God to guide you, lead you, and continue to order your steps on the right path. Your best is yet to come as you stay committed to setting the atmosphere!

LEADERSHIP CORNER:

God has and is ordering your steps. It's as simple as that. The God of the universe is guiding you to your next level. Walking in God's ordered steps requires discernment and obedience. What is God nudging you to do? What desire keeps resurfacing? Look back at your life; can you identify moments when God ordered your steps? Where is God leading you now?

Leadership Lesson: Experiences are divinely ordered steps for your next.

Scripture Support: *Trust in and rely confidently on the Lord with all your heart, and do not rely on your own insight or understanding. In all your ways know and acknowledge and recognize Him, and He will make your paths straight and smooth [removing obstacles that block your way]. (Proverbs 3:5-6 AMP)*

26

ABIDE: TRUSTING GOD FOR YOUR "NEXT"

L ife has a way of unfolding in the most unexpected ways. We all know what it's like to have a plan for life and our future, only to experience what seems to be a derailment—one that takes us down a different path. Towards the end of my second year as the superintendent of a Pennsylvania school district, I planned to continue serving the schools, working with the community, and partnering with the local churches, which greatly supported the district. There was an increase in student achievement, a decrease in discipline, and the graduation rate rose from 76 percent to 92 percent. All was going well, and I looked forward to continuing my work as their superintendent. However, that's when my plans began to unravel.

At the end of the second year, following a series of tests, my husband and I received a call to meet with a team of doctors at Johns Hopkins Hospital.

As we sat in the doctor's office, amidst multiple text exchanges between me and staff, I heard the doctor say, "Chester, you have Lymphoma." As he explained the diagnosis and treatment plan, he noticed that I was still preoccupied with texting messages back and forth. "Do I need to contact social services, Dr. Wortham? I am describing something critical here, and your attention is required. If your husband does not get chemo, he will be gone in less than a year."

He had my full attention, and I knew that things would have to change. I knew I had to resign to support my husband's journey back to good health.

My family and I were now facing a health crisis, one in which we would have to rely on faith, prayer, and trust in God to get us through. But not only were we facing a health crisis, we were facing challenges all around. In the presence of my husband, I remained optimistic, but deep down I was worried about our next—our next income, our next mortgage payment, our car note…the next steps. "Lord, how are we going to make it?," I prayed. "Lord, we have two mortgages, and I don't have a job. How are we going to make it?" It was then that I heard a word deep within my spirit: "Abide." My first response was, "Abide?! No God, for real, how are we going make it?!" Again, I heard, "Abide."

As I sat with God, I was reminded of the scripture, John 15:5: "I am the vine; you are the branches; he who *abides* in me and I in him, he bears much fruit, for *apart* from me, you can do nothing." I was unemployed, but God wanted me to abide—to remain; to keep to; to make Jesus the focus of my life, not my problems. "Okay Deborah, you heard it. Abide." The fact was, I could not make it over this mountain of sickness and bills without God. I knew it, and God knew it, so I needed to abide.

Abiding in Christ reminded me of the teas that my husband

would make me before his diagnosis. He would put my favorite tea in a cup of steaming water and let it simply abide there. Eventually, the water will begin to transform into the color and flavor of the tea. The longer the tea bag stayed in the water, the darker the color and the stronger the tea. The longer I abided in Christ, the more I reflected God's peace, and the stronger I became. The more I abided in prayer and God's Word—meditating on scripture, the more hope was restored. The more I abided in the preached Word—listening to it, and allowing it to seep into my spirit, the stronger my faith became. The more I abided by recalling God's promises, the more peace I experienced.

During those uncertain times, I granted God full access to my inner soul. Jesus became the center of my thoughts, my life's focus, and my heart's passion. Abiding in God and trusting God for my next was necessary for mental, spiritual, and even physical survival during that difficult time.

Things did not get better immediately; in fact, things had taken a turn for the worse when we met the doctor for a follow-up visit. We expected good news, but what we heard was, "You failed chemo."

Huh?! How does one fail chemo?, I thought. The doctor continued, "You have two options. You can go through eight weeks of radiation, or another six months of chemo, but you would have to be hospitalized." *Trust God, Deborah. Keep abiding.*

After a family meeting and much prayer, Chester made the decision to take the radiation option. I continued to abide and trust God. When he was not in chemo or radiation, I did consulting work one or two days per month. I trusted God for my next, and God was so faithful that by the end of the year, we were informed by our tax consultant that we had to pay more taxes than in prior years. Why? Simply because God supplied our next, and I made more as a consultant, working one or two days per month, than I did as a superintendent. The Lord provides our next!

On our next visit to the doctor, we received the news we were believing God for. Chester was healed from Lymphoma. We praised and thanked the Lord for God's faithfulness. A year later, I applied for a position as superintendent for another district in Pennsylvania and received an appointment. A few years after this life-altering experience, Chester received another unfavorable diagnosis. This time, it was prostate cancer, but I did not have to resign again. My family and I orchestrated a care plan for his weeks of radiation, and we abided and trusted God for our next. Once again, God was faithful, and Chester was healed. Since then, no matter what I've faced as an educational leader and in life, I'm reminded to abide and trust God.

LEADERSHIP CORNER:

Perhaps you are facing a major personal trial, or maybe you are in the midst of making some major decisions. *Do I do this, or do I do that? Do I take a leap of faith, or do I stay where I am?* Perhaps your prayer has been, "Lord, how are we going to make it?" Or, "Lord, should I take this job? Should I apply for this position? Should I leave now? What should I do?" If this is where you are on your educational leadership journey, or your personal journey as an educational leader, then I encourage you to abide and trust God for your next. What would that look like for you? What does *abiding* and trusting God for your next as an educational leader look like for your life?

Leadership Lesson: Abide and trust in the God who has your next.

Scripture Support*: "I am the vine, you are the branches. He who abides in Me, and I in him, bears much fruit; for without from Me you can do nothing." (John 15:5 NKJV)*

27

KNOWING YOUR "WHY"

"**D**eborah, go to your room."

My response, "Why?"

"Deborah, go and do the dishes."

I replied, "Why?"

"Deborah start doing your homework."

Again, "Why?" This was my constant response to instructions from my parents while growing up. I wanted to know why. I needed details—an explanation. I needed the why and even when my mom responded, "Because I said so!" I still needed the why.

This curiosity—the need to identify and understand the *why* has followed me throughout my leadership journey. My *why* fueled my passion and drive. My *why* kept me pushing beyond obstacle after obstacle. My *why* gave me clarity and direction. My *why* was and still is my restorative force—it will restore hope and vision. My *why* was my sustaining force—it helped to sustain the inspiration needed to keep moving forward. It was and still is my vitamin, providing me with the energy I need to not hit the snooze button for a second time. When one stands at the crossroad of decisions, it is one's faith and one's *why* that direct one's path.

As a leader, I've always found great joy in inspiring others to believe in their capacity to live a quality life and accomplish their dreams. Nothing gives me more pleasure than witnessing someone succeed in life. However, one of the things I implore all to do is define and redefine your *why* along the journey. Why do you want to move to the next level? Why do you want that position? Why do you want to work in that district? Why do you want to work at that school? Why do you do what you do?

I truly believe that when one's *why* is not properly identified and defined, the result is internal and external chaos. When the why is misplaced, lost, or forgotten, much like a password, it reflects in one's demeanor—we have limited capacity to deal with the daily trials; we are closed off, unapproachable, inaccessible, and sometimes we simply shut down mentally and emotionally. This is when we need a reset—a reset of one's *why*.

I am at the point in my career as a Superintendent where I can clearly see the fulfillment of my *why*. I see the manifestation of my *why* when students believe in themselves and transform their way of thinking. I see my *why* when the beliefs, practices, and protocols that I worked to put into place yield success for the students and schools. I know I am living in my *why* and walking in purpose when I hear the applause of parents, and the shouts of "Congratulations!" as graduate after graduate strolls across the graduation stage. Knowing my why has kept me moving from one level to the next. However, throughout my life and career, I have had to define and redefine my *why* as doors opened and closed. And sometimes when I simply need to stir up my *why*, I quiet myself and read this "Acceptance of the Class" statement. It stirs my *why* by reminding me that my efforts to set the atmosphere—enabling young scholars to become college and career-ready were successful and my labor was not in vain.

SUPERINTENDENT:

> *"In recognition of the certification of these graduates, recommendation by the Principal, and acknowledgment of the Board of Education; by the authority vested in me by the Department of Education as a Commissioned Officer, as the Superintendent of the School District, I take pleasure in certifying this Graduating Class for the conferring of high school diplomas."*
>
> *~Dr. Deborah L. Wortham,*
> *Superintendent of Schools (Setter of the Atmosphere)*

LEADERSHIP CORNER

Your next level will require you to define or refine your *why*. Take some time to think about what drives you—the driving force behind your ambitious goals. One thing I have discovered along the way is that faith and your *why* are your superpowers. Your *why* will give you the strength you need to keep pushing, keep believing, keep reaching, and keep moving. So, what's your *why*?

Leadership Lesson: Your *why* creates your vision, your vision stirs action, and your action propels you into your destiny.

Scripture Support: *"For I know the plans and thoughts that I have for you,' says the Lord, 'plans for peace and well-being and not for disaster, to give you a future and a hope." (Jeremiah 29:11 AMP)*

28

OPPOSITION TO POSITION

I've been honored to be the recipient of many leadership awards. I've been blessed to serve various districts throughout the United States. I know what it takes to take a district from "school improvement" to "good standing." I know how to move from one level of success to the next, but I also know what it's like to face opposition on the ladder to success. As you move to your next, know that opposition is inevitable. It may come in the form of an uncooperative board. It may be in the form of fabricated and malicious reports. It may come through anyone and at any time. However, when they do come, keep the faith, and trust God through the process.

As I look back on my journey, there were several instances when I completely had to trust God to make it through opposition. I distinctly remember the battle I faced as the new superintendent of a particular district. It was while I was serving there that a website was created for the sole purpose of dismantling my character, tarnishing my credibility, and stunting the success of the district. God delivered me from that attack, and I succeeded in my efforts to serve that district with all twelve of the K–8 schools rated as "good standing."

But just when I got over one hurdle, I was faced with another.

Upon leaving that district and going to another district, I was faced with opposition in the form of letters written by an anonymous community caucus to the secretary of education, the Regents, the NAACP, and other large organizations. This opposition was intense since it involved stakeholders and several notable organizations. Again, God delivered, and I was reminded that when God is on your side, you have victory, even if the world is against you. When I left that district, all five K–12 schools were in good standing.

Most recently, during the COVID-19 pandemic, I was faced with opposition when, upon my arrival as the new superintendent of a district, I was welcomed with the absence of 140 teachers. For an entire year we had to remain focused and not allow the fight to distract us.

We stayed focused on instruction. The curriculum and instruction teams worked together with integrity, all while working tirelessly with the attorneys to bring the teachers and teaching assistants back into the building. God was with us, and eventually, all teachers and assistants returned. Following professional development initiatives and the implementation of the new curriculum, we successfully transformed all five schools within the district from "school improvement" to "good standing."

At this point in my career, I have come to realize that opposition is nothing but a veiled distraction. It aims to get you flustered, confused, and unfocused. Opposition of any type means that you are a threat to progress. It wants to stop you from moving to your next, derail you, frustrate you, and ultimately ensure your failure. But again, if God is for you—if God is on your side, then nothing or no one can successfully oppose you. With a growth mindset, you cannot and will not lose!

LEADERSHIP CORNER

As I pen these words, I am smiling at the thought of how God has vindicated me throughout the years and elevated me in spite of opposition. I'm smiling at a recent text received from the New York State Department of Education inviting me to meet with Deputy Secretary Melina concerning my successful innovations and initiatives throughout my career. Opposition will come as you move to your next level, but God will fight for you. God will give you wisdom and strategies. What opposition are you facing now that you need to surrender to God? What will you remain focused on despite the challenges?

Leadership Lesson: Opposition means you are a threat to progress. Stay focused!

Scripture Support: *"Have I not commanded you? Be strong and courageous! Do not be terrified or dismayed (intimidated), for the Lord your God is with you wherever you go." (Joshua 1:9 AMP)*

29

LEGACY LEADERS

Dear Dr. Wortham,

Good morning. I just wanted to share something personal with you to thank you. So, my whole life, I have never had a role model. I had a lot of people whose life I did not want to emulate. That's how I kept myself motivated. This applies to childhood through adulthood. But here I am at 39, realizing that you have become my role model. I've always looked to you, even when you didn't know it. You taught me how to be a Principal and how to cultivate a better mindset. So, one day when you leave this district, please remember that you have left your "mark" on so many lives, especially mine. Have a beautiful day.

~Ms. Carolyn Partridge

A s leaders, we are mentors to individuals near and far. Our lives—what we do, how we do it, what we say, how we say it, and when and how we show up—are living epistles (letters) read by many. Our style, stamina, and steadfastness are being observed and even emulated by others. If we serve well, we become lights, illuminating the path for others on their educational journey. As such, I've always been mindful of how I lead and serve district after district throughout the United States. I've always been mindful of the legacy I'm leaving behind as I move from one level to the next.

When I think about legacy, I think about leaving a mark of excellence, poise, and passion. Leaving a legacy of leadership means creating a positive culture, establishing an efficacious environment, situating systemic stamina, and activating an atmosphere for the achievement of students and staff, in every place that you serve. Effective leaders are legacy builders who recognize that legacy begins the minute we say "yes" to the position. They are visionaries who understand the weight of their decisions and how everything they do has the power to impact lives.

Legacy begins the minute you accept the new job, get a new title, start teaching a new grade, or start serving in a new district. Leaving indelible marks as we move to our next, means having a legacy mindset—one that is proactive and not retroactive—focused on healthy, positive, confident actions moving forward. So, as you move on to your next, here are some tenets to ensure that you leave a positive mark:

1. ***Self-Evaluation:*** I truly believe that true growth occurs when we can be honest with ourselves about areas in our lives where we need some improvement. Take some time and write down 5 areas in leadership and rate yourself on a scale of 1-10, with 1 being "needing the most improvement," and 10 being 'mastered.' These 5 leadership skills may be: Motivation, Conflict Resolution, Relationship Building, Empathy, and Communication, just to name a few.

2. ***Invite Feedback:*** Who are your trusted advisors? It is so important that we not only surround ourselves with people who celebrate us when we glow, but also with individuals who will help us to grow. Seek feedback from those individuals who have your best interests at heart and want you to be the best that you can be. These are individuals who will critically challenge you, while strengthening your confidence. Ask them to rate you on the leadership skills you chose. Why? Because sometimes we can't see ourselves objectively—we have blind spots. Having trusted advisors who are willing to provide honest, affirming feedback will help us become better leaders in our next. Whoever these advisors are, make sure they are not "yes" people, and that they function in diverse roles within the organization.

3. ***Make The Change:*** We can't change what we did yesterday, but God willing, we have the power to change how we will show up tomorrow. Now that you have done

some self-evaluation, and invited feedback from others, it's time to do the work. How will you show up in your next position? There is always room for growth. Create a vision for how you want to lead moving forward. Create a vision for the legacy you plan on leaving in your next.

For several years, the title, *Setting the Atmosphere* remained on my desk, in my drawer, on a frame, in my bookcase, in my wallet, or in my Bible. It was a constant reminder that the success I sought for others or myself was within my control. Fifty-six years later, I now know that it was through prayer, faith, and favor that the manifestation of my sister Lori's words, "Be the best that you can be," became my reality.

I became the best I could be because I was legacy-focused. Legacy is never about us. For me, it was always about a deep desire and commitment to serve, surrender, and secure sanity and sanctity. As you move to your next, stay focused on God, keep the faith, humble yourself to receive guidance, do the work of self-improvement, and know that God is not through with you yet—the best is yet to come. Continue to serve, continue to grow, continue to lead, and continue to set the atmosphere!

What does legacy look like for you, and how can you set the atmosphere of leadership legacy—one that moves you to your next, all while making room for others; empowering others to see their greatness, and helping them to chart their course?

Leadership Lesson: Legacy leaves a mark of excellence, poise, and passion.

Scripture Support: *"A good name [earned by honorable behavior, godly wisdom, moral courage, and personal integrity] is more desirable than great riches; and favor is better than silver and gold." (Proverbs 22:1 AMP)*

PART 6

CONCLUSION

30

PERSEVERE AND PUSH: IT'S NOT ABOUT YOU

"**D**r. Wortham, I do not have anyone else to talk to!" Sarah, one of my favorite students from elementary school (now a senior in high school) was distraught. "Okay Sarah, come in and let's talk about it."

With clearance from the security guard, Sarah entered the double doors to the Central Office and made her way to me.

"Dr. Wortham, students are having a difficult time as they go through this pandemic, and many are suffering."

Sarah was a passionate advocate who was concerned about the state of her fellow students. "Dr. Wortham, we need to do something to help." I listened intently and asked her to provide the names of the students that she was concerned about. I expected her to name about five students, but Sarah began to name student after student. "Wait, stop!," I exclaimed. Moved by her passion, I responded, "Wow, that's more than I thought! We must do something for the entire graduating class."

During our time together in that office Sarah and I shed tears as I told her that I wanted her to be on the podium on graduation day to help me place red stoles around the neck of every graduating senior. We decided on red stoles because that color signifies *power, alarm, and alert*. For us it represented the strength and perseverance of the students as they pushed forward to graduate. We wanted these students to know that we saw them, and we honor them.

Tears flowed as Sarah opened up about how difficult life had been. At the time, her mother was hospitalized with cancer, and she was working several jobs while her mother fought the disease. I marveled at how selfless this young lady was and told her that we will tell her story and share her passion with everyone on graduation day.

It's not about us. It's not about you and it's not about me. This call to serve as educational leaders is a call to selflessness. Amid her struggles, Sarah was concerned about others. If we are to serve with excellence, we must take the "me mentality" out of the equation. This journey is one that's replete with difficulties, challenges, and struggles, and yet we must not lose sight of our "why." In spite of our personal dilemmas, we must be compassionate, empathetic leaders who hears, sees, and is concerned about the overall wellbeing of each student.

On graduation day Sarah's story was told and her passion felt as she assisted in placing stoles around the necks of 267 graduating seniors. Her mom mustered enough strength to attend and was seated directly behind the graduates in a section seemingly reserved for her. Sarah beamed as I acknowledged her mom who waved both hands at the mention of her name. I will never forget that wave and the halo over her.

One month after graduation, Sarah's mom passed away and went home to be with the Lord. Sarah wore her red stole to her mother's homegoing service. In that moment the stole represented the memory of her mom's shining moment as she witnessed Sarah use her voice to make a difference in the lives of the graduating students. In essence the stole was a transference of the servanthood mantle, as Sarah walked in her mom's footsteps who was a highly active student advocate, volunteer, and leader within the school district.

As I reflect on this final story, I am so happy that I did not dismiss Sarah's concerns or view them as trivial. That day and the moments thereafter were divinely orchestrated. Sarah's selflessness and passion represent all that I aim to be as an educational leader. When I reflect on how God used me to help Sarah empower her fellow students, my sister Lori's decree comes to mind, and I am brought to my knees. "Deborah, be the best that you can be."

I heard you Lori and will continue to be the best servant-leader that I can be. My labor has not and will not be in vain.

Selah.

LEADERSHIP CORNER:

Finally, my fellow educational leader, put on your red stole. Put on your strength, persevere, and push forward. You are a servant leader and as such, it's not about you. You are called to pour out, empower, educate, uplift, and positively impact students' lives. How you show up for one child has the power to change that child's life and generations to come.

Leadership Lesson: Your labor is not in vain.

Supporting Scripture: *"Let each of you look not only to his own interests but also to the interests of others."* *(Philippians 2:4 ESV)*

THE APPENDIX

Transforming Schools: Powerful Strategies to Propel Schools from "Improvement" to "Good Standing."

The following is an exploration of strategies that have proven to be game changers in my career, propelling schools from a state of "school improvement" to the coveted status of "good standing." Throughout my extensive experience, I have honed a set of non-negotiable strategies that have consistently played a pivotal role in the transformation of schools.

These strategies are not mere suggestions, but rather imperative directives that have the potential to revolutionize your educational institutions. They have been carefully crafted and refined, drawing from a wealth of knowledge and practical wisdom gained from years of dedicated service.

I encourage you to embrace each strategy wholeheartedly. They have been communicated to principals with great urgency, as each one is deemed essential for implementation. However, I also invite you to adapt and tailor these strategies to suit your district's unique needs and circumstances. Flexibility is key in ensuring their successful integration into your educational landscape.

Together, let us embark on this transformative journey, equipped with specific and actionable strategies that will propel your schools towards excellence. Remarkable changes lie ahead as we navigate the path from "school improvement" to "good standing."

1. Follow-up on taking daily attendance.
2. Announce and view (by all) the Superintendent's morning message. Confirm that all staff can access the message.
3. Employ collaborative grouping of desks (4's) and

collaborative teaching.

4. Employ *"The Gathering"* – standing in the middle of the hallway during transitions (all administrators and staff...this takes as many people as possible).

5. No hallway passes for students to run errands.

6. Pre-approve daily lesson plans.

7. Ensure implementation of the systemic template for bulletin boards. (4 samples of student work, learning target, and rubric. Papers are dated and not ever older than 30 days.)

8. Ensure the Subject, Skill and Learning Target are on the board.

9. Mandate that all students wear school-designated uniforms.

10. Spend 50-75% of your day in the classroom talking about instruction (not in the office).

11. Develop an Annual Professional Performance Review (APPR) Observation / Evaluation Schedule.

12. Eliminate all clutter (offices or classrooms).

13. Organize and keep unused rooms organized.

14. Establish a college and career culture.

15. Create a hospitality office suite.

16. Provide one-to-one electronic devices (laptops) for each student and staff member.

17. Maintain a current website.

18. Provide no seats in the main office for student detention. Students must remain in their classrooms.

19. Teach the curriculum from bell to bell.

20. Ensure that Proficiency Partners are operable.

21. Ensure active student/teacher engagement.

22. In the case of class disruptions, teachers are to call the office and an administrator must go to the classroom.

23. Ensure the maintenance of hallway displays as follows: Samples of student work, learning target, and rubric; picture in the hallway (Elementary students); student names on sentence strips with papers inserted in sheet protectors; papers are dated and no more than 30 days old.

"WORTHAMISMS"

*W*orthamisms is a collection of educational leadership truisms that emerged while conducting Cabinet meetings during my tenure as a superintendent. These sayings, which I fondly refer to as "Divine Directives," came forth spontaneously during our discussions and were quickly recognized by my Cabinet members as valuable principles for implementation. As a result, they diligently recorded these sayings, ensuring their incorporation into our educational leadership practices. These *Worthamisms* encapsulate the wisdom and insights gained from years of experience and serve as guiding principles for fostering excellence in our educational institutions.

1. Do not indict on perception.
2. Titles make you think you're entitled.
3. Brand a unified community.
4. Swap programs for practices.
5. Leadership isn't something you are, it's something you get.
6. Divorce yourself from the drama.

7. Your pushback doesn't determine my future.

8. The principal is the pilot, controlling the direction, altitude, and attitude of schools.

9. Fly above the turbulence.

10. Speak the truth – save each other.

11. Time to inhale, not exhale. We have more work to do.

12. If your presence does not make a difference, then you're ineffective.

13. Suspension is not an intervention.

14. If you can see it, you have direction.

15. Talk your way to proficiency.

16. It's OK not to know. It's not OK not to know and not to learn.

17. Find Them, Teach Them, Send Them on Their Way!

ABOUT THE AUTHOR

D r. Deborah L. Wortham is an educator, best-selling co-author, elder, professor, and nationally recognized lecture circuit presenter. A native of Chicago, Illinois, Dr. Wortham is prepared spiritually and educationally. She is the former Superintendent of the School District of the City of York in York, Pennsylvania, and the Steelton-Highspire School District in Steelton, Pennsylvania. She was the first locally elected Superintendent of the Roosevelt Union Free School District in eleven years. During her tenure, the district moved from "State Takeover" to "Good Standing." Dr. Wortham served as the First African-American

Female Superintendent of the East Ramapo Central School District in Spring Valley, New York, where all 12 K-8 schools reached "Good Standing." Still fond of the Roosevelt Union Free School District; currently, Dr. Wortham serves as the Superintendent in charge of "Resetting Roosevelt!"

Her credentials include a Doctorate in Educational Leadership from Nova Southeastern University, Fort Lauderdale, Florida; a Master's Degree in Reading from Morgan State University, Baltimore, Maryland; and a Bachelor's Degree in Elementary Education from the University of Wisconsin, Madison, Wisconsin.

Dr. Wortham is a best-selling co-author of STEM Century: It Takes a Village to Raise a 21st Century Graduate. She received Elementary Teacher of the Year and Dissertation of the Year. Dr. Wortham is featured in several educational videos, has written numerous chapters for various books, and has traveled extensively, lecturing on various topics. Her most recent community highlights include the Top 100 Most Influential Educators in New York State; East Ramapo "Sheroe" Award; the Martin Luther King, Jr. Service Award; Rockland County School Board Association Award of Excellence; Mid-Hudson School Study Council, Educational Leadership Award; First Timothy Christian Church for Outstanding Contributions; and Leadership Award, Nassau County, New York NAACP. Additionally, the following awards: Washington Rose "Inspiring Woman" Award; Service Above Self Award, Central Nassau County of Rotary International; Salute to Unsung Sheroes' of Sisters in the Struggle Award, Nassau County; Educator of the

Year, Long Island Black Educator's Association, and the Sojourner Truth Award, Central Nassau Club of the National Association of Negro Business and Professional Women's Clubs, Inc.

Her national and international affiliations include being a life-member of Alpha Kappa Alpha Sorority, Incorporated, Theta Iota Omega Chapter; member of The Links, Incorporated, Long Island Chapter; Chaplain, National Coalition of 100 Black Women, Long Island Chapter; member of Rotary International, and a Life Member of Girl Scouts, PTA, and the NAACP.

Dr. Wortham has been married for 50 years to Rev. Chester H. Wortham, Jr. She and her husband work together in ministry locally and abroad. They have led marriage and leadership development seminars at various conferences. Dr. Wortham and her husband have two children, Dr. Shelley and Min. Chester, III; one son-in-law, Sheldon; one daughter-in-law, Marquita; one granddaughter, Jordynn Lynn; and four grandsons, Chester, IV, Sheldon, Jr., Zachary, and Ethan.

Dr. Wortham was licensed and certified as a Minister by the Board of Examiners, and in 2011 she was ordained as an Elder at the Higher Dimensions Christian Center in Baltimore, MD. "To God Be the Glory, for the Great things He has Done!"